PITS and PRAISES

Marianne Swenson

12.77

PITS and PRAISES

Glorianne Swenson

"Just when we think life is the Pits Lord,
You lift us up, and we Praise and Thank You
for that marvelous, upholding gift ~ of a lift!"
glori

WestBow
PRESS
A DIVISION OF THOMAS NELSON

WestBow Press books may be ordered through booksellers or by contacting:

WestBow Press
A Division of Thomas Nelson
1663 Liberty Drive
Bloomington, IN 47403
www.westbowpress.com
1-(866) 928-1240

Because of the dynamic nature of the Internet, any Web addresses or
links contained in this book may have changed since publication and
may no longer be valid. The views expressed in this work are solely those
of the author and do not necessarily reflect the views of the publisher,
and the publisher hereby disclaims any responsibility for them.

Any people depicted in stock imagery provided by Thinkstock are models,
and such images are being used for illustrative purposes only.

Certain stock imagery © Thinkstock.

ISBN: 978-1-4497-0726-2 (sc)
ISBN: 978-1-4497-0778-1 (e)

Library of Congress Control Number: 2010939285

Printed in the United States of America
WestBow Press rev. date: 01/07/2011

FOREWORD AND ACKNOWLEDGMENTS

•◆•

The pleasure I get from writing creative non-fiction is what makes my heart happy, but my writing would be worthless if I did not share it with others. I believe my writing is a God-given gift, and that He has a plan and a purpose for me. I'm excited about where He's leading me next in this art form.

Much of my writing reflects "the way things used to be." I feel it is important to pass these memories on down to younger generations so they can appreciate where they've come from. The thing I miss most about "the way things used to be" is the closeness of the family unit; the value of family, friends and neighbors working together to make the world a better place.

•◆•

May your days be filled with making someone's life more bearable—more sweet.

May you have a quiet day in between the must-haves of life—like filling an empty salt shaker or reading a book curled up under a blanket.

Even though the sun may not shine through the clouds for a week, we know that it will someday, and we hold on to that!

And when we stumble, let's make it part of the dance, because no one but God knows who choreographed the scene.

•→•

~To the keepers of my dreams over the years while waiting for my thoughts to formulate.

~To my encouragers who believed in me from the time the idea of a book was conceived.

~To the people in my life who contributed just by living their lives in a clear crystal bowl, allowing me to see their stories form on paper.

~To those who were waiting to hold this book in their hands who have already left this earth, but rejoice anyway as we prepare for the biggest book signing event in heaven.

~To my God who picked me up when I was discouraged, and hung around to see the dream come true.

~To those who entered my life quietly and let me share their joy, their pain and sorrows; knowing that their story was important to me.

~To my family and friends, doctors and nurses, teachers and clergy who kept telling me to keep breathing even through serious illnesses because the book needed to be finished. But then is a book ever really finished when there are still stories to be told.

~To those who realize that one has to put the period someplace..................

~To God for a sense of humor and a heart filled with passion.

~To the times I've been moved out of my comfort zone; for learning there are two days in every week that should be kept free from worry and fear. One of those days is yesterday, and the other day is tomorrow.

~To the times I have not missed out on a blessing because it wasn't packaged the way I expected.

Contents

•◆•

1

•◆•

Resolutions

Today I will burn a candle and bask in the fragrance of spiced
   apple.
I will take a nap between fresh sheets and not set the alarm.
I will laugh aloud even though there is no one else to hear me.
I will step out in the rain and feel the freshness of spring.

Today I will send a card and tell someone, "I love you."
I will climb hills and fly kites in the March winds.
I will cry at the movies and wish on a star.
I will pray for loved ones, for my country, and the dignity of
   man.

Today I will run through the tall grass like a giraffe, with my
   head held high.
I will read Shakespeare, Dr. Seuss, and Erma Bombeck all in
   the same day.

I will cradle a soft kitten in my arm and let my soul vibrate
with its purr.

I will drink amaretto flavored coffee and eat too much
chocolate.

Today I will write love songs, and dance like a child.

I will chase butterflies, rainbows and sunbeams.

I will walk in warm, white sand, and let the breeze blow through
my hair.

I will walk in the woods and pick wild violets and strawberries.

Today I will ride carousels and eat cotton candy.

I will send flowers to a friend and read to the blind.

I will write poetry and listen to music.

I will take a bubble bath and shop for lingerie.

Today I will rise early enough to see the moon set and the sun
rise.

I will drive in the country and remember myself as a child.

I will wear pink ballet slippers, perfumed talc, and 14k gold.

I will play in fall leaves and taste the first winter snow on my
tongue.

Today I will touch more. I will feel the unmatched softness
of a baby's skin.

I will hold a weathered hand of a friend in the sunset of her
life.

I will hug the grieving and feel their pain with them.

And if tomorrow never comes, I will have had today—and
touched the hand of God.

2

· ◆ ·

Autumn Highlights

In Minnesota, we are blessed with four very distinct seasons, but my heart is most in harmony with autumn.

As a child, autumn meant returning to the one-room country school. The two-mile walk on dusty gravel roads gave me time to appreciate some of God's creatures as they scampered or slithered across the path of small feet. Grasshoppers and monarchs seemed to be taking one last look at the warm days and changing environment. The school smelled of fresh varnish and new books, and the warm country breeze—soon to be crisp—blew through open windows. The walks home again brought flocks of noisy blackbirds descending on cornfields—soon to be harvested. Halloween brought trick-or-treating. Bobbing for apples in a galvanized tub of cold water brought smiles to our faces, some as toothless as the jack-o-lanterns we had carved earlier. Hayrides on cool nights brought out jackets, warm mittens, and laughter. Piles of raked leaves provided soft landings for small bodies.

As I grew older, the intoxicating smell of burning leaves and wood smoke from fireplaces permeated my clothes and my senses. The crickets putting their summer songs to bed, birds heading south, and squirrels gathering acorns for winter storage signaled a time to prepare for the long, hard, cold days of winter ahead. The sound and sight of ducks and geese flying overhead brought hunters in camouflage jackets, and meals to our tables. Roadside stands of freshly canned jams, jellies, and pickles harmonized with the harvest of pumpkins, gourds, cornstalks, Indian corn, bittersweet, and shafts of wheat, enticing the passerby to stop a moment in the fast pace of life and reflect on the bounty of God's earth. Crimson sumac silhouetted against a deep blue sky; golds, oranges, and reds mingled with browns and leftover shades of summer greens painted a picture like no other artist than the work of our Creator. Even the smallest bush or weed came alive with brilliant color as it put on its autumn coat.

Today I walk on wooded paths; the sound of leaves crunching and dry twigs snapping under foot remind me that these days are short lived, and this season of autumn and Thanksgiving will soon close its eyes and succumb to the early snows. And as one season blends into the next, I am blessed with the knowledge that autumn will return in its due season.

3

• ◆ •

District #247

School District #247. One room. One teacher. Eight grades. The smell of fresh varnish and new books when school began. The freedom to learn.

Were those days of the one-room schoolhouse really that great? Yes! Those eight years provided me with sweet memories for the rest of my life. I can only wonder how my life might have been different had I gone to school in the city.

Perhaps it was the two-mile walk along country roads early on a crisp fall day—listening to sounds that escaped many kids from the city. Perhaps it was blackbirds and robins in spring, rehearsing their Minnesota song on the telephone lines that rose from the ditches. Perhaps it was the little creatures that scampered or slithered across the road frightening little people feet.

Rural school—where teachers and students often became best friends. Where gifted education courses were provided for everyone just by listening to the class ahead of you being taught in the front of the room. And tutors were readily available for all ages by asking for help from the eighth-grader sitting next to you. For me it was sharing eight years in a class of two with a boy named David, singing duets with a girl named Donna, and the familiar sound of the bell in the tower being rung by a thick, braided rope to signal the start of classes again.

"Dick and Jane" books taught us how to read, and flashcards sharpened our math skills. Huge maps were pulled down from rolls fastened to the wall to teach us about faraway places and the geographical layout of the land. A single row of bookcases, filled with knowledge and adventure, comprised our library in a corner in the back of the room. Responsibilities were assigned to us taking turns heating up the hot lunch, passing out the milk, emptying wastebaskets, or cleaning the cloakroom. Responsibilities also included erasing the blackboards and pounding erasers on the school steps to clean them at the end of the day, with chalk dust flying into the air to make room for the eraser to do its job the next day. Responsibilities could be fun!

Industrial and fine arts every Friday afternoon honed in on the skills of all the children. Whether it was sawing boards to build a birdhouse, hammering a nail on a piece of metal to make a picture or a tray, or learning to embroider or paint, every child had a strong sense of artistic expression.

Pennies were brought to school to buy Easter Seals and Christmas Seals—one penny, one seal. And dimes were brought for the March of Dimes drive to help crippled children.

The hot lunch program consisted of last night's supper leftovers in a covered fruit jar, warmed to perfection in a dishpan of hot water on a two-burner hotplate.

October brought Halloween parties in the darkened basement, with spooky sounds and imagined scary visions. Peeled grapes, chicken liver, and cooked spaghetti slithered in our hands as stories of ghosts unfurled. Bobbing for apples brought laughter, as wet faces and hair emerged from the galvanized tub of cold water, desperately clenching a bright red apple between sparkly white teeth. As if that wasn't enough fun, in the evening, parents drove carloads of masked and costumed kids from one farm place to another for trick-or-treating, being treated with everything from popcorn balls to apples to sandwiches to candy and hot cocoa.

My siblings and I were the second generation of Andersons to be educated in District #247. When our generation started school, a fuel oil tank had replaced the coal bucket. We were fortunate to have a furnace to warm the school when I started first grade in 1949, even though we still used a wood stove at home. Outhouses gave way to chemical toilets in the school building during our generation—long before we had indoor plumbing at home. The old hand pump over the well provided our water until that too gave way to modern running water in the school building. It was a big day when we got a refrigerator at school, and the milkman began delivering half-pint cartons of milk for the students.

The teacher took inventory at the end of the school year, including the number of trees on the property! Requests were also made for the next year: a new water fountain, new floor, blackboards, chalk, erasers, window shades, a new porch, a large globe, a doormat for the hall, new textbooks and library books. The needs were simple, but often the school board needed a little urging to get them. Budgets were tight, and money was hard to raise.

Rural schoolteachers often spent the winter months in a neighborhood home, so they could be close to school. Our family had the privilege of providing room and board to Miss Langseth for a couple of years, and she became a treasured part of our family.

Skiing on wooden skis with leather straps across our boots, sliding on wooden sleds, and playing King of the Hill in winter brought rosy cheeks, snow-covered mittens and hats, and four-buckle overshoes back into the cloakroom at the back of the school when the bell rang.

Perhaps the greatest of all the rural school experiences were the Christmas programs. The huge tree was trimmed by all, stringing popcorn and cranberries and handmade paper chains made of red and green construction paper. The fathers built a stage out of planks and saw horses, and a black curtain was strung across the front of the stage for dramatic openings and closings. Schoolwork was often set aside temporarily while weeks of practicing songs, recitations, monologues, and plays culminated in the Christmas program. With desks shoved aside and planks supported by chairs, the room was filled with parents and siblings and neighbors. There was the year that I portrayed Yogi Yorgenson in "I Yust Go Nuts at Christmas," nearly wiping out the globe ceiling light with my cane in my robust enthusiasm, and the year I sang "Silver Bells" with my friend. The evening always ended with opening gifts that had been wrapped carefully and secretly tucked under the huge tree. The mothers served lunch, and Santa came with treats for the children, with everyone guessing who was behind the jolly white beard that year.

Horses and sleighs or cutters driven by fathers brought students back and forth to school when the winter weather was tough. When the winter snows began to melt in spring, family cars were left at ends of muddy driveways, while tractors carried children in trailers or wagons out the long driveway—all in an effort to get to school. At the end of the year, children with perfect attendance received awards.

Drop-the-handkerchief games brought squeals of laughter and gaiety in spring, and wooden teeter-totters and chain-link swings carried us high in the sky on our circus through life.

"Tour" came in springtime. It was a day when all eight grades were driven in cars by brave mothers the ten miles to town to experience the marvelous things of the city. We visited the Coke plant, watching the sweet syrup being poured into bottles that were capped by machines, and listening to the clicking rhythm of automation. At the *Journal* we watched the daily paper being typeset and then printed by huge, noisy presses, the smell and grime of newsprint reeling around us. At the county museum, we would admire the ways of our forefathers, and at the county jail, we tasted loneliness and fear when the cell door locked behind us, and tears came quickly. When the jailer unlocked the cells in short order, we experienced the gift and relief of freedom—never to be forgotten.

Spelling bees tested the academic skills of the children as we gathered with other rural schools to compete. Field days offered prizes and ribbons to participants in three-legged and gunnysack races, broad jump, high jump, and running and throwing skills. A festive potluck picnic was always prepared by the mothers for all to enjoy. Music festivals brought all the rural schools together in the city high school for singing, with weeks of rehearsing assigned songs preceding.

In the spring we brought our rakes for clean-up day. And when the work was done, a softball game came as a reward, followed by hotdogs and marshmallows roasting over a bonfire of sticks and leaves. Hotdog buns were sliced with a jackknife that had dissected a "friendly creature" earlier that day by a boy named Bobby.

Drowning gophers was a favorite of the boys at recess and before or after school, and sometimes they convinced the girls to carry the pail of water to pour down the gopher hole while they waited with their weapons in anticipation of the gopher coming out. The township offered a bounty for gopher tails—a penny a tail, but the boys did it just for fun, not profit!

PTA meetings included children at every meeting, and we listened and learned *ROBERT'S RULES OF ORDER* without opening the book. The meetings always ended with a big lunch for everyone—truly a family event. Once a year the PTA would host a basket social to raise money. The fair maidens of all ages would bring a beautifully decorated box of delicious lunch to share with the gentleman who made the highest bid. It was a time when stomachs became queasy with excitement or dread for who you might have to eat lunch with! The PTA hosted carnivals for fund raising, with fish ponds and cake walks, and games.

Rural education taught us responsibility, hard work, and good character. It taught us to care and to share. It instilled in us good study habits and friendships of all ages to last a lifetime. Those were the days when we saluted our country and prayed in the same breath—without repercussions. It gave us pleasant memories to fill the lonely days of old age.

4

•◆•

Daffodil

I grew up in a Norwegian Lutheran farm family. We had farm fresh roast beef, mashed potatoes and gravy, homegrown garden vegetables, homemade bread and red Jell-O with bananas and real whipped cream direct from the cow to the kitchen. And we prayed when no one else was looking.

I suspected that our neighbors across the duck slough lived similarly. Our barns shared opposite sides of that slough, and I figured the Leabo family cream came direct from the cow to the kitchen as well. As the crow flies, our farms were very close. But to actually get to one another's homes, we would have to go the long way around on the bumpy and winding Aurdal Township gravel road. That's where David lived.

Life is a journey. David's journey began in 1943. My journey had begun just three months before his. David and I started school together in the first grade. I like to say we skipped kindergarten, even if there wasn't any back then in the one-room rural school—District #247. We were the only two students in the class when we started first grade, and we were the only two when we finished the eighth grade. We studied, played and grew up together. Sometimes the teacher would let us go out to the cloakroom and study—if we didn't get into too much mischief. And David made sure that I wasn't the last one chosen for Prisoner's Base or the ball team!

I was always twice as big as David was. In pictures I usually had my arm around him—perhaps protecting him because he was so small. Perhaps it was because he couldn't get his arm around me!

Many days of our life journey were spent walking and talking along the bumpy gravel road from the end of my driveway to the school. He would come as far as my driveway, and then we would walk together. We listened to the birds sing and learned to recognize them by their call. We watched the little creatures scamper and slither across our path as we walked. And we talked about the signs of spring to write on the blackboard in the back of the room when we got to school. It would only be right that we would have nicknames for each other. He called me Googie-Ann. I called him Daffodil.

Most vivid in my mind was David's first bicycle. My first bike was a blue Schwinn. David's first bike was a yellow Donald Duck bike with a life-like image of Donald Duck at the front. The bike was small, because David was small. I waited at the end of the driveway to hear the beep-beep of his horn coming around the bend of the gravel road.

David and I shared our Christian faith as we attended Sunday School, Luther League, and confirmation together in the Lutheran Free Church. I remained true to the Lutheran doctrine, while David fell in love with a Methodist. It didn't matter. We both loved and worshipped the same God, and Christ was at the center of our lives.

And so the journey went on. After our marriages to Wayne and Darlene, we both lived in Fargo/Moorhead where Wayne and David attended Moorhead State University together to become what they wanted to be when they grew up!

People ask me, "Why didn't you marry David?" And my answer is, "Because he asked Darlene!"

Money was tight in those early marriage and college days, and we often got together in each other's apartments for food and fellowship. Darlene will be the first to tell you that we ate many tuna fish sandwiches as we spent time together as couples.

As our families grew, it became a tradition to gather with other friends at the Leabo home on New Years Eve. We sat by the fireplace, played games, and ate—always ate. And we kept in touch in many other ways.

In February of 2000, David, Darlene and I said good-bye to our dear friend and high school classmate, Karen Ringstad—at the Grace Methodist Church. Little did I know that a year later, I would be in the same church saying my last good-bye to David. On the day of Karen's funeral, we stood in the narthex of the church visiting with friends, and David was wearing a patch over one eye to help with a recently developed double vision. We listened as he told about the scheduled visit to Mayo Clinic the next week to confirm the diagnosis of cancer. I reached out and hugged him, explaining that I wanted to hug him now in case I didn't get a chance again. I stood, holding this small man with the big heart in my arms for a moment, as Darlene and Wayne and our friends had a good laugh. And he said, "That was a good hug!"

As the cancer progressed, I had another opportunity to hug him on Thanksgiving weekend 2000 at their home. And once again he said, "That was a good hug!" And we reminisced about growing up and about our grade school teachers.

And then we prayed together—he, clutching my arms tightly. I knew that our Lord would be coming soon for my friend. So I prayed for the perfect healing and the perfect peace which is only found in Jesus Christ our Lord, and shared how we look forward to that day with joy and anticipation when we will see Him face to face.

God answered our prayer. David is now enjoying the fellowship and joy of being face to face and side by side with Jesus. Heaven shines brighter today because he is there.

If he were still with us today, he'd be concerned about the Israeli-Palestinian conflict, the war on terror, and the starving children in the world. He would be doing his part locally by ringing the bell for the Salvation Army kettle and distributing Bibles with his fellow Gideons. He would still be Papa to his grandchildren and loving Darlene.

Oh, when people looked at him, they visualized a small man. But if people knew him, they knew he was one of the biggest men they'd ever known. He had a big heart and a huge capacity to love other people—especially his family. And his love for Jesus was wider than any ocean.

And on my journey through life, I was blessed to know him. I miss you, my little Daffodil.

5

·◆·

Privy Information

Growing up on a farm in rural Minnesota certainly lent itself to numerous ways of life not always understood by city folks in the 40's, 50's, and 60's. Not the least of these being—the outhouse!

Although the family outhouse on our farm may have looked like the traditional two-holer, our outhouse was a deluxe model. As you opened the door from the outside, there to your right was a special third hole, just the right size and height for the little people. Obviously, privacy wasn't an issue in those days since three holes side by side offered close proximity to a friend or sibling in their most private moments.

Our outhouse was nestled in the trees across the road from the house. The outward weathered appearance faded into the natural landscape of trees, grasses, weeds, and brush. A small, wood door latch on the outside of the door kept the door from blowing in the wind and prevented uninvited creatures from entering when not in use. A metal hook locked the world outside while we attended to the necessary matters of life and maintained our privacy from the inside. Two small, round openings loomed on either side near the top of the outhouse. Serving two purposes, the openings let in your only source of light as well as providing a primitive form of air conditioning and venting.

If properly built, the sitting holes would have wooden covers which lifted off when in use. What this prevented, I'm not sure! It only made me wonder what was down there waiting to come out as I sat down.

Piled on the floor or between the holes were an assortment of newspapers, magazines, and catalogs. They not only offered low cost sanitary wipes, but wonderful reading material as well. The soft black and white printed pages were used first, leaving the hard, colored, glossy covers and pages for emergencies only. The *SEARS ROEBUCK* and *MONTGOMERY WARD* catalogs, *THE FARMER*, and *FAMILY CIRCLE* magazines became intimate friends.

The cold Minnesota winters did not allow for reading time in the outhouse. But hot summer days with flies buzzing incessantly around you and spiders spinning intricate webs of beauty in the sunbeams provided more sitting time and more reading time.

Then one Sunday in 1951 our family of five, plus grandma and grandpa, piled into two vehicles and headed down old Highway 52 the 60 miles to Fargo, North Dakota. That's where great aunt Julia lived. Great aunt Julia's life had not always been easy, and she and her family had endured their share of primitive farm life. But the latter years had been good to them, and now their farm on the edge of town had been slowly growing into a housing development. Julia had indoor plumbing—a toilet that actually flushed! Aunt Julia would always share a portion of her abundance with our family when we came to visit. Often grandma would come home with a set of new sheets, a beautiful new tablecloth, towels, or a silky night gown fit for the finest of ladies. Often these gifts went into grandma's cedar chest, for they were just too good to use!

But this day was different! When we were ready to make the long trip home, Julia took us down the basement. There it stood, a white porcelain privy. Never had we seen such beauty on the farm! We stood there in awe, and then smiles broke out over our faces. This throne was fit for a queen! The precious cargo was carefully loaded into the car, and we headed back down old Highway 52 to Fergus Falls.

The porcelain privy was tenderly placed in what soon became known as the "little room." No, there was no handle to flush. There was no running water. A heavy porcelain removable insert with a heavy braided rope attached, was lifted out as it reached its upper limits of capacity. The removable insert was then carried outside to the slop yard across the road. It was my mother's privilege to care for this gift, this modern convenience that we now proudly owned. The Hilex jug and the old aluminum tea kettle filled with boiling water accompanied my mother out to the back porch as she labored over the cleanliness of the glamorous white object. Now shining like white diamonds in the sunlight, it was carried inside and took its place again inside the porcelain privy in the little room. More Hilex was poured into the prize container, and we were free to use and appreciate it once more.

Along with the porcelain privy came the advent of white paper on cardboard rolls, but the reading material was still piled high on the floor for those who chose to linger.

Indoor plumbing on the farm didn't become a reality until after I was grown, married, and enjoying my own private facility in the city.

Recently, we were in the process of redecorating our second bathroom downstairs in our home. Preparing for the men to lay new floor covering, my husband removed the toilet and carted it out to the screened in porch. And then I heard a crash! I looked, and before my eyes lay a pile of gray porcelain in pieces. I was soon to learn more than I ever wanted to know about toilets, as we began shopping for a replacement.

Brand names began buzzing in my head, and choices of flushing systems became dinner table talk. There were as many models to choose from as there were flies in the outhouse. Materials ranged from cast acrylic to vitreous china to cultured marble. Styles and colors were available to suit any décor and space configuration, and prices to fit any budget. Toilets were now described as virtually inspiring, bold, made for the soul, and styles you're in love with. We searched for toilet availability on the Internet, in the local stores, and made long distance calls to other towns. We had our choice of a standard fixture or a state-of-the-art model. We became acquainted with hydraulically engineered trap ways, sanitary dams, valves, bowls, and quiet refills. I dreamt about choices of rough-ins, tanks that were insulated or not insulated, one-piece or two-piece toilets, space saving round fronts or elongated models for extra comfort, and prices. Never before had my mind been so boggled with privy information.

We had discovered that a toilet is a very personal fixture. Just when we thought we had found the premium toilet that would suit our needs and desires, we were confronted with the fact that toilets do not automatically come with seats and lids. Now we started our search for the perfect design and color to match the toilet. We concerned ourselves with hinge designs, finger lift options, high or low gloss finishes, solid plastics, or oak wood.

I took a deep breath, and found myself yearning for the simplicity of the outhouse, with the flies buzzing and spiders spinning webs in the sunbeams. Life was so simple then. Or was it?

6

•◆•

Carefully Starched

Her name was Tillie. At home my mother referred to her as *"Tilla."* With a decided Norwegian brogue, she would emphasize the *"Till"* part. It was easy for her to jest. She was my Dad's sister, not hers!

Aunt Tillie had remarkably pale, white skin with large patches of brown pigment. As a child I thought she looked like a giant piece of lefse. In spite of her large boned, tall and lean body, I thought occasionally that I could see her sternness melt slightly with a soft smile or a twinkle in her eye. I genuinely liked this meticulous, careful lady. She was deeply religious, and I soon learned that I did not talk about seeing a movie, playing a card game, or working on Sunday in her presence.

Tillie was married to a gentle, soft-spoken, kind-hearted man. There were no children in their lives. Her house was spotless and carefully arranged, and I knew when I visited her that I must sit properly on her very proper furniture and remain quiet and polite. I surmised that whatever musical talent I had probably came directly from this aunt. She sat proudly on her piano and organ benches as she commanded the keys and pedals to respond to her interpretation of the notes on the page. Her back was straight and her arms and fingers were directive and arched appropriately as her voice trilled and vibrated to her own accompaniment. Each piece of sheet music was eloquently labeled for ownership—"Tillie Caroline Twedt." Never had "The Lord's Prayer" or "Beautiful Isle of Somewhere" been treated with such dignity and respect.

Each blade of grass in her yard stood at attention and the carefully placed flowers in the weedless beds seemed to glow with perfection and pride. Baseballs did not land in her yard. Children did not frolic and play there. Stray dogs and cats knew her boundaries even without fences or signs. She was an accomplished seamstress with never a stitch out of place. The garments she wore were starched and flawless. Dust mites did not live in Tillie's house. In fact, one questioned if anything truly lived in Tillie's house!

Her large, bony hands crocheted quickly and rhythmically. The hook danced gracefully with the thread as it transformed into beautifully created doilies—soon to be starched with the same exactness that symbolized this stately lady. I knew I could count on a new doily each year for Christmas, carefully wrapped in tissue paper in a very proper box. Even now, her doilies adorn my furniture. The stiffness is gone, replaced now with the beauty and softness that had always been there but had seldom been seen through the starch.

And now I know that much like the doilies, there was a certain beauty and softness about her soul—only masked by the outward appearance. And sometimes—just sometimes, the starch came out, and her mouth softened in a smile and her eyes twinkled.

7

•◆•

Rehearsal for Life

Perhaps they grew them different on the Montana-North Dakota border. Perhaps it was because his large, calloused hands spoke of working with the earth or the fact that he knew how to milk a cow. But when I brought Wayne down to the barn to meet my Dad, I knew there was instant approval.

My cowboy soon became the Rock of Gibraltar in my life. His family became my best friends and encouragers. My life as an 18-year-old was fast becoming entwined in a different flavor of mid-western life with hills and valleys, family, friends, and laughter.

Two months of a whirlwind courtship led to proposal of marriage on February 2, 1962. The fact that it was Groundhog Day didn't seem to matter. Could it have waited until my birthday, February 6 or the romantic Valentine's Day? No, not for the cowboy. He was ready to propose—and we would forever share this day with Punxsutawney Phil.

Asking my parents for my hand in marriage came with an exuberant blessing, but with the request that I finish my technical school—one and one-half years down the road. These were the days when respect for and obedience to parents were not only expected, but also demanded. So we waited.

With both of us coming from less than prosperous farm families, Mother Gyda gave her engagement and wedding ring diamonds to her only son to have rings made for her only daughter-in-law. Picking out the settings together at Welander's Jewelry, the bill came to $25.00, and the cowboy had to make payments of $5.00 a month.

Soon separation would engulf our relationship as he took a break from college to work on the family farm, and later as a construction worker leveling land. The cowboy, the farmer, the "cat skinner"—they also talked different out there.

Time passed. A year and a half with little money and 485 miles of North Dakota prairies and badlands between us. A few short visits and the art of letter writing kept us focused on July 14, 1963. I had grown into a 20-year-old woman, and Wayne was now a mature 21.

Preparations were carefully and conservatively made. My mother gave me $20.00 to buy my wedding dress—mission accomplished. And though I dreamed of a bridal bouquet filled with yellow roses, it became instead a small colonial bouquet of three yellow roses surrounded by mums and greens. The 14-karat gold wedding band for the groom arrived from the Spiegel's catalog for $14.00.

It was a Sunday afternoon. The mid-summer heat accompanied July 14 as we made our way to the little white country church.

The organist played the familiar "Here Comes the Bride," and we were pronounced man and wife by the officiating preacher. The sanctuary of the little church was crowded and the reception was celebrated in the even smaller, musty-smelling basement with cement walls and floor. The aroma of egg coffee, boiled in large enamel coffee pots, competed for air space. With the huge metal furnace as a focal point, it spread its ductwork like a bloated octopus, furnishing the backdrop for wedding pictures of cutting the cake. And the festivities continued—first, at the church; and then, at the farm.

With no money there would be no honeymoon. But my mother had arranged for us to spend the night in a small cottage by Fish Lake, which bordered the farm. The time came for us to leave—now in my going-away, white, sheath dress and high heels. We unhooked the manure spreader from our decorated car which was up on blocks. We drove down the long driveway and came in the back dirt road and across the fields and pastures to the little cottage. No one but our folks knew where we were.

Morning came. I awoke with an excruciating headache. Then I sat up on the edge of the bed. The room was spinning. I felt too faint to get up and go to the next room and get aspirin from my purse. I woke up the cowboy to help me. The obliging groom got up and immediately went to the next room, and then I heard a loud crash! The cowboy had fainted and hit his head on a sturdy metal lawn chair.

"Something is wrong," I surmised. I forced myself to get to the other room, and I dragged the semi-conscious groom out on the cottage steps and propped him up against the wall. Now he sat there, staring into space.

I knew that if I didn't hit the trail to the outhouse, I would lose my wedding cake right there, so I went down the trail in my red negligee—a gift from the cowboy.

I returned, feeling better. "Wayne, you have to get your pants on," I announced. I was seemingly the only one in control now so I went into the cabin and grabbed his pants and my purse and helped dress my cowboy.

I knew that this man could not drive. So I stuffed him in the passenger side of the car, and I drove through the wooded path and pastures and gate up to the farmhouse.

Now, the cowboy's folks had stayed at the farmhouse overnight with my parents. It was 6:30 a.m. His mother, being an early riser—as farm folks tend to be—was standing on the back porch as we drove up in our still decorated '57 Chevy.

By this time, I had completely lost control over my emotions. I stopped the car. The cowboy got out of the passenger's side. I got out of the driver's side in my red negligee, carrying my large, white purse and weeping hysterically.

My new mother-in-law stood with her face ashen and her arms gesturing, and shouted as if the cowboy were still on his rocking horse, "Wayne, what have you done to her?"

Upon investigation, the gas refrigerator in the cottage was found to be faulty, leaving the air filled with carbon monoxide gas. Our brains were oxygen deprived!

The doctor was called. He said we would have terrible headaches for a long time and should postpone going to our new home in Montana for a few days. He prescribed pain pills and bed rest and said that the worst thing that could happen was brain damage. That certainly left us reassured!

Lucky to be alive, you say? No, blessed to be alive! Something good often comes out of something bad. If I had not woken up with that nasty headache, we would not be here to tell you about it today.

God, from the moment of conception, has a plan and a purpose for us, and He chose for us to live to fulfill that plan and purpose. Oh yes, there have been hills to climb and rivers to cross, but God is always with us, holding our hands, weeping with us in our sorrows, and sharing our joys. We have learned that the earth has music for those who listen and that all things are possible for those who love the Lord.

8

• ◆ •

Tears for Jonathan

It was 1966, and things were going according to plan. We had both worked hard to get to that point—I in my job and Wayne in his education. College graduation would bring an end to the old life, and the beginning of a new life.

Marriage, education, jobs, children, hopes and dreams. Winter was turning to spring, not only on the calendar, but in our lives as well.

I was working in a medical facility as an x-ray technologist, and Wayne was looking for his first teaching job. He would graduate in May. The news of my pregnancy was an expected joy as we continued to put the pieces of the puzzle of life together.

In our hearts, we knew that our baby was a boy—a son to carry on the family name. We decided to name him Jonathan Wayne.

As only a mother can experience, the bonding had taken place from the moment of conception. This relationship was so deeply mine.

April came. Easter weekend came. The beginning of my fourth month of pregnancy came. We set out on our journey to southern Minnesota for Wayne's first teaching interview. I knew it would be a long ride, but the early symptoms of pregnancy were waning. I would be fine.

The interview was a positive one although we would wait for God to give us a peace about it. We were half way home again when I started to hemorrhage. No one had prepared me for this. Perhaps the ride had been too long; the excitement too much.

By the time we arrived home that Good Friday evening, the hemorrhaging and cramping had grown worse. I called my obstetrician. In his cold, matter-of-fact way, he told me to go to bed for 3 days, but that I would probably lose "it" anyway. He spoke of my baby as if he were an object, not a human life. I was pregnant with a baby, not an onion! This man was getting on my nerves. I went to bed.

Saturday evening came and the signs of miscarriage were becoming more evident. Every alarm in my body was going off! My whole system was rebelling! I was too weak and faint to stay in the bathroom alone, so Wayne stayed by my side. The decision was made to go to the hospital; I could no longer deal with this trauma at home.

I looked at the murky water. Not recognizing anything as tissue, I flushed the toilet. I collapsed in Wayne's arms, and he carried me up the stairs from our basement apartment and into the car.

From the emergency room I was rushed up to the OB floor. I don't know who admitted me because I never saw a doctor.

Easter Morning came—a day of new life and new hope. I still hadn't been examined by a doctor. I questioned the nurses. Was I still pregnant or had I miscarried at home? They had no answers for me.

On Monday morning, my obstetrician examined me and told me that I had miscarried. He asked me what I had done with the remains. I told him I didn't recognize anything as remains. I hadn't saved anything. Then he spoke harshly to me, "That's like committing a murder and hiding the evidence!"

Guilt and shame flooded my entire being. "Now we'll have to do a D and C to make sure that all the tissue was expelled," he said sharply and callously.

"Oh dear God," I thought, "I flushed my baby down the toilet!" Instead of birth, death had come—involuntarily, suddenly, and unexpectedly. Canyons of sadness consumed me. How could I deal with this emotional pain? The doctor made me feel like it was my fault. I stuffed my feelings. I didn't allow myself to grieve. He made me feel cheap and bad.

The D and C was performed. I felt empty and alone. I was discharged and went back to work the next day. There were no pictures to share. No footprints. No handprints. There was no funeral or memorial service. There was no body for burial. No one brought over a casserole.

No one said anything. It was 1966, and no one openly talked about miscarriage. My own family didn't even talk about it. It was an intensely personal loss that no one was able to share—not even my husband. I decided I would not feel anything. I would amputate grief at the neck!

Wayne accepted a teaching job in my home town. October came. My once anticipated due date arrived. My friend and neighbor gave birth to a beautiful baby girl. I refused to feel the pain and emptiness of my own loss.

At Christmas time, I was pregnant again. Our son Mark was born in 1967. Twenty-one months later, our next son Kurt was born. Four years later we were blessed with our baby girl Jennifer. All pregnancies were normal, and our children were healthy, bright, and beautiful.

Years passed. It was 1993, and I was working at a funeral home. I was helping people cope with the loss of their loved ones. I had also worked for hospice, facilitating grief support groups. I had attended many seminars to help prepare me for this special ministry.

It was time for another seminar—"Practical Ways to Help When a Baby Dies." I listened intently as the presenters talked of neo-natal death—miscarriage, pre-mature, stillbirth, and after the birth. They spoke of the loss of a dream. They spoke of fetal disposal laws and recognizing the grief process.

As I sat there taking notes, the presenter began to speak about miscarriages that are flushed down the toilet. "The body goes down, but the spirit exists and continues to live with our Creator," she said. My mind raced back 27 years. Out of nowhere the pain enveloped me. Rivers of tears flooded my soul. Someone had finally given me permission to grieve the death of my baby Jonathan. She gave me permission to release all the emotions I had stuffed for all those years. Waves of grief came crashing over me.

When the speaker was finished, she came and put her arms around me, and others comforted me as well. I told them my story, and they listened and understood. They encouraged me to name my baby and have a memorial. I had already named my baby in my heart, but I had been embarrassed to share this with family and friends.

The tears were a cleansing agent for me. My heart began to heal. The cracks were still there, but as time passed, the spaces between the cracks became less visible. In 1999, Wayne and I planted an apple tree in memory of Jonathan Wayne. Each year I watch it grow tall and slender and filled with spring blossoms—soon to bear fruit. It speaks of his life. His life was short, but it was life, and he was loved. Jonathan may not have walked this earth, but he was someone. He had a soul, and he is in Heaven. I will see him some day.

9

· ◆ ·

Granny B.

Whenever I need comfort, my thoughts turn to Granny B. She was someone who believed in me. She taught me much about life. This spring I planted pansies in memory of my Granny B., and I remembered.

Moss roses, pansies and peonies! No one else could raise them like she did. Peonies had always highlighted her flower beds, blooming in all their majesty, elegance, and fragrance. White, light pink, medium pink, dark rose, singles, doubles. I can still sense the sweet aroma that filled her house when she picked a lovely bouquet and placed them in a plain fruit jar to grace the top of the old oil burning stove in the summer.

I learned a lot about peonies, moss roses, and pansies from Granny B., but I also learned about the beauty of a baking powder biscuit. They were like cumulous clouds that melted in your mouth. Yet, in my kitchen when I followed her recipe, they descended off the pan like rocks down a mountain slide.

Her instructions for cooking and baking were exact—exactly frustrating, that is! A pinch of this, a handful of that. Bake cookies long enough so they don't fall apart when you lift them off the cookie sheet. "How long would that be?" I pondered. So that's the way I learned to cook. Now when my kids or their spouses ask me for a recipe, I say, "Oh, I don't have one. Just throw in whatever looks right, a handful of this and a little of that!" And I smile and remember.

I also learned love and patience and good moral values from Granny B. She taught me to be a good mother, a good neighbor, and about being a friend. She watched "Days of our Lives" on TV, but assured me that those things didn't happen in real life!

I don't recall that she ever had a Christmas tree in her tiny house by the levee, nor do I recall any particular monetary or material gifts purchased at that time of the year. Although I'm sure there were, those weren't the things I found important as I grew up. Instead, I savored the warmth and character of my grandmother, a lady who I lovingly knew as Granny B. As Christmas drew near, the boxes of homemade sandbackles, rosettes, and lefse seemed to pop up everywhere. We could sense the sparkle and enthusiasm that surrounded this beautiful lady.

She was Grandpa B's mate, of course, and they lived in a cozy little house in Fergus Falls, Minnesota. It was so close to the high school that they could almost hear the choir sing, and they loved to watch and listen to the marching band practice on the levee.

I spent much time with my Granny B. I often spent several days at a time at her house as a child. Later I lived with her and Grandpa B. for six years when school was in session. Living in town was a convenience that allowed me to take part in more activities and friendships than if I stayed at home and rode the bus. On weekends, vacations, and summers I returned to the farm.

Granny B's upstairs was my bedroom. It was one big room with a tiny closet where I hung my clothes, and a crawl-in attic that stored long ago treasures. I can still hear the lonely sound of the train whistle on the nearby tracks as I lay in the old iron bed, trying to fall asleep. And then a sweet peace came over me, and I drifted off to dreamland.

Grandpa wasn't a big conversationalist, so often we would eat supper in silence. When we finished eating, he would migrate to his big chair in the living room. Then Granny B. would say, "Put your feet in my lap," and she would rub my feet and try to straighten my crooked toes. And we would spend some precious time in conversation. That was one of the many heart gifts that she gave to me.

I learned much from her gentleness, orderliness, and cleanliness. I embraced her love of housekeeping. She taught me to sew, to rip, and to make perfect on her old Singer treadle sewing machine.

I inherited my aches and pains from Granny B. With rheumatism raging through her body over the years, she could often be seen with a hot water bottle wrapped in a towel, soothing a sore spot. I braided her long, blond, naturally curly hair before she'd go to bed at night when the rheumatism wouldn't let her arms up high enough to do it herself.

I can still hear the crackling of the oil burner in the living room. I can still smell the scent of the special bottle of French perfume—tucked away in a little box with a special hanky.

Her son had sent them to her when he was in World War II. I recall the hairpins she used to get her hair rolled up neatly and the garters that held up her nylon hosiery at her knees. Vivid in my mind is the struggle she endured to get her one-piece corset on if she was going some place special, the sweat pouring down her body.

Each day she could be seen with her nylon mesh grocery bag in her hand, walking briskly across the levee and up the big hill to Charlie and Inga's Lake Alice Grocery for our daily bread. When my brother and I got to go along, we would be treated to a banana or root beer Popsicle for the price of a nickel.

"Just one more cookie won't make you fat," she'd say as she passed the sandwiches and goodies over and over again. The coffee brewed on her stove time and again, always ready for company to come and sit a spell.

In the evening, her voice would call me to wash her back in the bathtub. Oh, it was a small payment of love for all the sacrificial things she had done for me. Her pendulous breasts, broad hips, and the turned down corners of her mouth even when she smiled became mine as I grew older. And her Norwegian spunk taught me to stand tall in the face of adversity. If human cloning had been possible, I would have suspected that I was my grandma! Yes, we were soul mates.

Granny B. went to be with her Lord in 1977. Now I know the cumulus clouds really are her baking powder biscuits as my eyes look toward the heavens.

Years have passed. I am a grandma now. My own precious granddaughters are my new soul mates. Whenever they need comfort, I hope their thoughts turn to me, because I believe in them. And I hope they plant pansies one day and remember.

10

•◆•

Unlocked Memories

"Come Boss! Come Boss! Come Bossy!" My father's call carried through the warm Minnesota summer air, bidding the cows to come home for the last milking of the day. Whether they had spent the day grazing in the green pastures or had wandered to the lakeshore for a drink of water or to cool their bodies against the wet, sandy soil, they knew his call. And they came. Their udders swayed back and forth in a pendulous motion, heavy with the smell of fresh, warm milk.

As the wheels of the car hummed along the highway through the beautiful countryside, many things triggered memories of my father. He was a strong, yet gentle man. Though often not verbal, he taught me much about life just by the way he lived. Although much of his instruction was by example alone, he was specific in certain things—like when I learned to drive, "Never cut corners, and never drive over 40 mph on a gravel road."

He knew the sun, the rain, and the power of the wind better than most folks did. I remembered the winter of '68 -'69. Snow banks towered on both sides of the car as we drove "over the river and through the woods." That winter Dad made a road across the plowed field because there was no more room to push snow.

I never knew as a child that there was any stigma attached to wearing feed sack dresses. I would proudly go to the granary and pick out the colorful material for new clothes—two sacks for a skirt and one for a blouse. I never minded carrying in water or wood, or even taking a bath in the galvanized tub by the wood stove in the kitchen. There was a lesson to be learned about not going in debt or being extravagant. "Always pay cash," he said.

As I drove through the lush countryside, I saw more and more things that reminded me of my father. Windmills, that no longer provided a cool drink on a hot day, towered over the trees and buildings. I reflected on the creaking sound of the windmill in the otherwise silent, dark, night on the farm. I remembered the metal cup hanging from a wire on the windmill that Dad would fill with cold, refreshing, well water.

Grain heading out and waiting to be harvested brought a smile to my lips as I brought the mental picture of the threshing run into focus. It was *his* threshing machine! How excited I was as a child to see the crew move out like a great parade on its way to another farm. The big iron machine was followed by puffing, old tractors pulling grain wagons and hayracks. As I remembered, I could almost feel the chaff down my back and hear the elevator engine putt-putt-putting away as the grain was shoveled into its enormous jaws and carried into the bins of the granary.

Threshermen were hungry men! Lunch was brought out to the field twice a day as well as the men coming to the house for a big meal at noon and at the end of the day. Huge enamel pots steamed with the magnificent aroma of coffee. Thermos jugs filled with grape or cherry Kool-Aid and ice were carefully packed into the old car. Big blue roasters filled with hearty sandwiches and homemade cakes and cookies accompanied the women and children of the house as the car meandered slowly over the rough dirt roads and bumpy fields. In the field, blankets were carefully laid out on top of the straw stubble, and the food was spread out for all to enjoy. The men in their bib overalls, with sweat pouring down their bodies, took breaks from the puffing and clattering machines and 90 degree heat to restore their energy. And I was thrilled to have lunch with my father.

Sunday was a day of rest in the Lord's eyes, and in my father's eyes as well. We did not work on Sundays—except to care for the animals and provide nourishment for our bodies. Our day began with worship at the little, white country church a few miles down the road. When we arrived home again, we shared together as a family the farm fresh roast beef, mashed potatoes and gravy, home grown vegetables, homemade bread, and red Jell-O with bananas and real whipped cream. And we listened to "The Lutheran Hour" on the old kitchen radio—a reinforcement of what we believed the Lord's day to be.

On Sunday afternoons we enjoyed long, relaxing rides through the countryside to see how the crops were doing. Windows wide open with our hair blowing in the breeze,

Daddy kept time to his own music as his foot tapped gently on the gas pedal—up and down, up and down. The tires hummed and thumped like an orchestra in the background. Then we'd stop for a nickel ice cream cone at the country store, even though nickels were hard to come by. I never knew we were poor, because he made my life seem rich.

No matter how busy, he found the time to help with that special 4-H animal project or take us to the church for Luther League. He loved his animals. He loved his land. He loved his family.

Daddy always had a tune on his lips, humming or whistling, and I could even hear him above the drone of the tractor in the field if the wind was just right. He loved it when I'd play his favorite songs on the piano, and he would sing along.

My father never spoke harshly to me. He sometimes gave me a bad time if I cleared the dinner table before he was done eating. But I could always tell when he was joking because he got two deep lines between his eyes when he was trying to keep from laughing. And when I grew up, he approved of my choice for a husband, and he loved our children, teaching them to love the outdoors, the land, and the creatures that God had created.

In May 1985, a rare blood disorder that soon turned to leukemia, made him weak and tired. Dad had been a farmer all his life, and his last wish was to plant his field of wheat. Too weak to lift the bags of seed up into the planter, my mother did it for him. Then he carefully got on the tractor and planted the tiny seeds in the rich, black soil. And I could hear a soft whistle above the sound of the tractor.

Being of Scandinavian descent, our family was not accustomed to saying, "I love you." The night before my father's 72nd birthday, I knew we wouldn't have his physical presence much longer. Tears came to his eyes as he slowly opened his carefully chosen presents. I took his hand and said, "Daddy, have I ever told you how much I love you?"

"Oh yes, many times," he replied. He knew that he was loved even if we didn't verbalize it.

During those last few days in the hospital, I was privileged to be near to him and strengthen the bond between us—a silent bond. I was there to say, "I love you Daddy." I was there to hold his hand and wipe the sweat from his brow as his life reached out to its conclusion.

How appropriate that he was born in May—this man of the earth and fields and furrows. How appropriate that he found eternal life in May as well.

When harvest time came, I walked through the field of wheat he had planted that spring. I plucked some stems of wheat from the ground and gathered them in my arms to bring home. The wind was just right, and I was quite sure that I heard a soft whistle.

11

The Empty Barn

In the prime of her time,
she stood red and tall,
the hub of activity on the farm.
Sheltering animals, their home, of course,
the old barn stood the test of time.
She stands there now with signs of age—
a piece gone there,
a piece hanging there.
Her back is swayed
and aches in the wind;
a mere skeleton of what she once had been.

The red of her youth now stands
weathered and worn;
the haymow empty
and the barn door gone.

She used to resound
with the laughter of children,
the warmth of the cattle,
the meow of the kittens,
and the whistle of the farmer
as he earned his living.

She's seen hard times
and good times—life and death
within her rough and beaten boards.
Orphaned lambs no longer bottled and cradled
in this cathedral building called a barn.
Empty troughs wait for the contented chewing
and mooing of cows;
no longer heard,
but still remembered.
A barn swallow breaks into her emptiness—
her loneliness.

She's so much more
than beams and rafters.
She's the bridge of time
linking past to present.
She's a symbol of what farming's all about—
this barnyard castle, this holder of memories.
If I stop to listen,
I'll hear the tales of the farmer,
his wife, the children, and the weather.

Her sides used to ache

with newly mown hay;
drawing children to her loft
with whispers of adventure.
Cats with their kittens
found refuge in her secret places.
The sound of new birth
cried in her arms—
brought joy to her soul
and tears to her eyes.

The years have gone by,
the children are grown.
The sounds are gone,
but still she remembers.
Bats bump in the night
against her aching frame.
No gathering of flies now;
no cows to bother.
No swishing of tails or
cleaning of gutters.

She moans and groans;
her old weathered bones
raging in the storm—
no longer the protector of life
she used to be.
The morning sun rises
and spiders spin webs
in the sunshine peeking
through the cracks in her frame,

but the rooster doesn't crow.

Her owners have died
or moved into town.
Her foundation has crumbled
with the elements of time.
Her hair is thinning
and her sight almost gone;
her stanchions abandoned,
and nothing in her stalls.
Pieces of straw still scattered on her floors,
make nests for the barn mice in fall.

She will stand there alone
until the death of time takes
her to new and unknown places.
As city folk drive by they say,
"Look at the old barn. It's funny
someone doesn't tear it down."
Her battered window now hangs
in the young lady's kitchen,
adorned with silk flowers and ivy.
Her boards are now benches,
birdhouses and signs, welcoming
friends to her new place in time.

12

·◆·

The Fisk

I'm not sure what the origin of lutefisk is, but I have a few theories.

First, it sailed across the ocean from Norway with my great-grandmother and her four small children. They poured lye on this ancient fish to make sure it would survive the trip, and it splashed all the way from Norway to the United States.

Second, in his youth my Grandpa Braaten was a lumberjack in the northern woods near Bemidji, Minnesota. One day as he began work, he saw a fish lying on a log. He picked it up, threw it in a wooden rain barrel, and four years later the camp cook served the first lutefisk to the lumberjacks near Bemidji.

Third, on the farm where I grew up there was a dark, damp cellar with a dirt floor and stone walls. Two sets of stairs led to the cellar; one from the outside through the wooden cellar door and another from a trap door in the pantry off the kitchen. Strange things were known to be lurking in that cellar. Far in the corner of the musty smelling cellar was a small room devoted to potatoes. As the winter months merged toward spring, tentacles grew—not unlike those of an octopus—out of the eyes of the potatoes. Lizards slithered to and fro across the floor, and a common sight was my mother going down the stairs with shovel in hand to ward off the slimy creatures. So naturally, when the lutefisk appeared in a kettle on the pantry floor shortly after Thanksgiving every year and sat there until Christmas Eve, I knew that there was also lutefisk living in the cellar.

Fourth, my faith in God has always been very real to me. As a small baby in the early 1940s, my mother would lay me in the pew while she taught Sunday School, played the piano for small voices to sing "Jesus Loves Me," or presided as Sunday School superintendent. I began learning Bible stories at a very early age. One of my favorites was how Jesus fed the 5,000 with five loaves of bread and two small fish. Twelve baskets of broken pieces were left over. I always wondered what Jesus did with the leftover fish. My belief in the Bible story was reaffirmed and my question answered when they started serving lutefisk at the Lutheran church suppers.

Now that we have a variety of origins to choose from for the smelly fish that surfaces mainly during the holidays in our Minnesota community, I must admit to you that I have never eaten lutefisk. My father hated the disgusting fish, and I loved and respected my father so much that I wouldn't think of eating the dreadful dish. From the time it appeared in the kettle on the pantry floor, the poignant aroma permeated not only the pantry, but also the entire house. You see, we had to leave the pantry door open somewhat in the winter or things would freeze in there. I don't think anyone was terribly worried that the lutefisk would freeze because anything that shook like a bowl full of jelly would be hard to kill by freezing, and anything that smelled that bad was probably already dead.

And so, for whatever reason, lutefisk became a tradition at our table on Christmas Eve when I was growing up on the farm. It was served with melted butter and boiled potatoes. Those of us who chose not to have our stomachs look like the tarnished inside surface of the kettle in which it was cooked, were offered meatballs and mashed potatoes. It was the Lutheran thing to do! As if they didn't get enough of the Scandinavian delicacy on Christmas Eve, it was offered again on Christmas morning in creamed form. Grandma and Grandpa and Mother rubbed their full tummies and a look of supreme satisfaction settled over their faces. At last, the remaining bones were cleaned up by the cat. The debate over the origin of lutefisk continued each year, and I could almost hear a verbal rivalry between the lutefisk and the meatballs as they each took their place on the appropriate plates.

When I married and had children of my own, Christmas Eve was celebrated at our house with my parents and grandparents joining us. I thought that now I might be freed of the lutefisk tradition. But no, mother would arrive in plenty of time with her own kettle to boil the water to cook the lutefisk herself. What was even more terrifying to me was that my husband actually ate the stuff and soon my oldest son learned to love it. I suspected then that lutefisk is very much like marriage vows—"for better or for worse, until death do us part!" As the years went by and our family grew and my grandparents passed away, I thought the meatballs might have a chance of winning out. I was wrong! Mother eventually quit bringing her own kettle, so now even my kettle was branded with the fisk. When my father died in 1985, I had no one left to defend me, and lutefisk still appeared on Christmas Eve. So I suffered in silence as I watched my silver-plated silverware tarnish at the touch of the fisk.

In the fall of 1987, my mother was diagnosed with cancer. She was very tired and weak, but she seemed determined to go grocery shopping with me one pleasant November afternoon. It was a chance for her to tell her story, so it seemed. Most people when asked, "How are you?" will lie and say "Fine!" Not my mother! She would stop her cart directly in the path of the person who greeted her and say, "Not very good. I have cancer you know." And her listeners would politely let her tell her story and then offer their condolences. I patiently waited through her story over and over again. She was slow and sad and had perfected her sigh, but her step seemed to quicken just a bit and a little smile came to her lips as we neared the meat counter—straight to the sign that said LUTEFISK! Oh, you could feel her joy as she spied the smelly fish laying in the display case. They had tamed down lutefisk considerably over the years. Instead of coming in a wooden barrel of lye, it now was delicately laid out on a Styrofoam tray, covered and carefully sealed with a thin piece of plastic wrap. It didn't even seem to jiggle any more.

Mother surveyed her find with much thought as she picked up a small tray of lutefisk—our fish lovers having decreased to 3 now, and put it in the cart. "We'll get it now so we have it for Christmas Eve," she announced. And I knew her silent prayer was, "God save the lutefisk!" We loaded up the small sacks of groceries, her appetite waning due to the cancer. When I unloaded my mother and her groceries at her apartment, she tenderly placed the lutefisk in my hands and told me to take it home so we could enjoy lutefisk for Christmas Eve. Once again the lutefisk joined me in my car, in spite of knowing that the odor could linger for weeks. When I arrived home, I carried it into my house with the same care I would carry a small baby in need of a diaper change. I knew I could leave it on the counter for the next couple of months and it would be fine, but instead I put it in the freezer, just in case we didn't get to the lutefisk for Christmas Eve.

Christmas neared and mother grew worse from the cancer. As she lay in her hospital bed now, we took turns sitting with her, going to Christmas Eve services with tears in our eyes and to Perkins for supper. No one ordered lutefisk. On January 7, 1988, two short months after the cancer diagnosis and the purchase of the lutefisk, mother went to be with her Lord.

The lutefisk sat in my freezer until Easter. Lutefisk cannot rot! Our oldest son kept asking for the lutefisk so I reluctantly took it out and cooked it—in my kettle, of course. The lutefisk did not jiggle. I don't think it even smelled. I couldn't see or smell very good through the tears. I set it before my husband and oldest son—now the only two remaining lutefisk lovers— and handed them the melted butter and the boiled potatoes. No one said anything. My appetite wasn't even there for the meatballs. And so, we said good-bye to the lutefisk and to a long tradition of teasing and taunting and debating the cause and the origin of lutefisk. From that day on, lutefisk has never been served in my home again. Lutefisk just wasn't meant to be there without my mother, who loved it so much. The two men in our family, who still associate by-gone Christmas Eves with the Fisk, now sneak down to the Viking Café or to the Lutheran church suppers to re-live their memories.

Even now as Christmas nears, I sense that God and my mother are smiling down at me as I ponder the question, "Will there be lutefisk in Heaven?"

13

⋅◆⋅

Maiden Voyage

She was one of the three Anderson sisters. I've been told that she had an opportunity to get married once—but when she found out he kept pigs in the house, she chose to take the "maiden voyage."

Life was a journey that started in 1903, and each day brought her a bit closer to eternity. The peaks and valleys of everyday life were becoming less prominent now, and the plains seemed an easier place to be. Her small, frail body revealed her 84 years. I had been helping her in small ways since her only living sibling was recently diagnosed with cancer, but now I became her primary caregiver.

I climbed the 18 steps to her small apartment at the top of the stairs. The strange, yet soon to be familiar sounds and scents emulated from the various apartments and culminated in the long hall to an almost stagnant, stifling sensation.

I knocked at Apartment No. 2 and waited for her slippered feet to shuffle towards the door. It was early morning, and I knew she would not be expecting company—not even me. She opened the door and stood there in her flannel gown, seemingly too much material for her tiny body. A pink, nylon ruffled nightcap gripped her small, tired face. Her mere 80 lb. seemed to border on anorexia. The thick lenses of the eyeglasses spoke of her legally blind eyes. The brewing of Oriental tea and the smell of mothballs permeated the hot, stuffy air in the room as we greeted one another.

I hugged her gently, feeling her small, thin, bony frame in my arms. I fulfilled my mission of telling her that her sister Florence had died. I could tell that hugs were not a part of her life, as she stood non-respondent, except for a few tears streaking down her cheeks.

I became her almost constant companion as I pledged to take care of her. Up the 18 steps, down the 18 steps—time after time, often accompanied by my husband—cleaning, laundry, errands, trips to the doctors and to the beauty shop, and trimming toenails and fingernails. Up the 18 steps, down the 18 steps, bringing small grocery bags only half full—tofu, one small apple, one small banana for potassium, a few potatoes, carrots, rice cakes, dark bread, honey, and tuna fish.

I gently washed the aged, white curtains, carefully sewed the ragged seams together by hand, and tenderly gathered the ruffles again. Up the 18 steps, down the 18 steps.

We looked at the same photo albums, over and over again. And she lovingly placed in my hands my great-grandfather Torgus Torgusson's Norwegian Bible dated December 11,

1893. The pages were brown and worn, and even though I couldn't read the Norwegian tongue, it spoke heavily to me of the Good News and of the days gone by.

Her presence became a tradition at our Thanksgiving and Christmas tables, and it was a delight to watch her eat and enjoy the food and fellowship.

She was a frameless picture, this Aunt Bella of mine. By day she would listen to local AM radio as she sat in her worn out, over-stuffed chair, or walked ceaselessly around her apartment and watched the world go by through her windows. Even though the wheels of the world seemed to have stopped for her, she peered through almost blinded eyes now as she watched her church next door, the traffic of life going up and down the street, and a small bird in the tree outside her window.

She opened her door a crack to see what was happening down the hall, leading to adjacent apartments. There was a story behind each door that concerned her, and she shared their colorful stories with me.

Two years passed, and evening would still find Bella sitting in her nightgown, her pills in her little blue container with spaces labeled Sunday through Saturday untouched, the food in her refrigerator growing rancid. The day was coming soon when I would be picking the art foam magnets off the refrigerator and throwing out the dusty, artificial flowers and other insignificant trinkets that seemed so important to her.

Days and nights became mingled. Flannel nightgowns shifted into daytime, and black oxford shoes shifted into nighttime. Time became meaningless. She now looked at me as though I was the one who was confused. Soon I would close the door to Apartment No. 2 and go down the 18 steps for the last time.

Transition to the nursing home was not seamless. She talked to God a lot, perhaps because He seemed old too, and she thought He understood old ladies better than ordinary folks did. Her old slippers were like a prayer as they padded across the floor of the nursing home—and He heard them. She knew there was a time and a season for everything, and she didn't worry about when He would come for her. She just knew that He would.

Another year passed and she was now struggling with cancer. Transition and time brought her to a bed in the hospital with tubes and oxygen. Her skin was as soft as angel wings. Now she took comfort in holding my hand. Yes, we had learned to touch, and it didn't matter that she called me by her dead sister's name Tillie. Eternity didn't seem that far away now. The chapters in her book were closing.

She had traveled life's journey, and death came as her friend that early January morning in 1991. The shrill ring of the telephone by my bed was a message without words. The maiden voyage was over.

A celebration of her life was planned. My siblings and I tucked her in and closed the casket at her church where she had once served so willingly on the kitchen committee, and folded bulletins faithfully on Fridays.

Trumpets sounded, and it was a service of rejoicing because she had gone home to live with her Lord. Yes, she knew He would come for her. And if one listened closely, the harps of a thousand angels could be heard in Heaven.

I can still hear in the distance her shuffling psalm of a walk. Wait—I hear a second set of footsteps walking beside her.

14

. ◆ .

Joy in my Heart—Peace in my Soul

I was 50 something, and my life was about to change forever. I didn't realize it at the time, but I soon learned that the journey I was on was part of the Master Potter's greater plan for my life.

In mid-November 1995, I was having a major flare-up of my fibromyalgia and chronic fatigue syndrome, but I kept pushing to get ready for the holidays. My life had been a series of health problems. I would get better, I thought. By January 1996, my illness was worse. I came home from work and went to bed. I could hardly lift my head.

The diagnosis came slowly. It was finally determined that I had eosinophilic pneumonitis in both lungs—P.I.E. Syndrome, a rare and serious autoimmune disorder. My doctor stood by my hospital bedside and told me that I had a 50/50 chance to live if my body did not respond to prednisone therapy. His words resonated in my ears. As I spent the day in prayer, it was the first of many times to come that I felt the gentle touch of angel's wings.

I knew no one else with this autoimmune disorder. Where would my support system come from? Community wings of prayer surrounded me as I fought to hold on to life. The medical staff urgently instructed and encouraged me to "Keep breathing—just keep breathing!" I clung to Jeremiah 29:11 (NIV) : *"I know the plans I have for you,"* declares the Lord, *"plans to prosper you and not to harm you, plans to give you hope and a future."*

I wasn't afraid of dying, but I was certain that I had too much living to do yet and that God still had plans for me here on earth.

Knowing that God uses us not only in our abilities, but in our disabilities as well, I set my mind to recover and live! I would shoot for the 50% chance of survival! God gave the doctors wisdom, and He gave me strength to fight for my life.

The years ahead brought countless more tests and visits to the emergency room, clinic, and hospital. Not only was the disease destroying my body, but the prednisone, which actually saved my life, was destroying my body as well. I experienced numerous side effects, some of which have affected my life forever.

Adjust, modify, and simplify were now part of my vocabulary. My business suits and uniforms were replaced with pajamas and robes. Naps became a necessary part of each day. Pain, pills, and breathing difficulties became my traveling companions. It was time to accept that I had a different lifestyle now. I would have to rebuild my body and my spirit in the process.

On November 1, 2000, I went off prednisone completely after five years. I am in remission. Even in remission, my health is less than perfect. I still take about 50 pills a day and use inhalers to aid my breathing. I don't know how long remission will last, but I do know that even in a set-back I will be able to see the other side of the mountain and press on.

With this disability, my life still has purpose. I am thankful for the gifts God has given me. I can still be a witness and strength for other people, and God inspired me to pursue my life-long dream of being a writer. I was determined not to die with the book still in me. So with pen in hand, I started writing. With God as my co-author, how could I go wrong? I was fitting into His plan.

I joined a writer's group for support and spent much time at the library researching the art and business of writing. Even though my first story was rejected, I decided that rejection was not a word in my vocabulary that would cause me to quit. So I plunged forward—writing and submitting. Soon I was a successful freelance writer, and I started my own small business.

My dance with life has new music now. I have learned not to get hung up on beginnings and endings, but rather concentrate on what happens in between. There are many things in life that I can no longer do, but I've learned to keep things simple. I only do today what I can do today. I try not to wish too often for the life I had. Instead, I put that energy into figuring out a way to make the life I have now a little better. I concentrate on the things that are possible for me to do, and I continue to find joy in my heart and peace in my soul. I am thankful for friends and family who encourage me, laugh with me, share a tear with me, pray with and for me, and love me unconditionally.

As long as I am breathing, and as long as I have life, I will be thankful for each new day and the hope and fulfillment it brings. I am thankful for the kind of days that are better than the bad days. When I wake up in the morning, I say, "It's going to be a great day!" And someday if I don't wake up in the morning, I'll know it's an even greater day!

15

•◆•

A Christmas Moment

It was 1997. As I sat at my dining room table, I wondered how I would ever get ready for Christmas. I was tired and weak, and every muscle and nerve in my body were screaming.

I looked out my window to see the sun shining and the grass still semi-green. It was already December 20, and this was Minnesota. We were hoping for snow!

Without getting up from my chair at home, I knew people all over the world were scurrying to finish their last minute preparations for Christmas. And then there was me. I was just beginning to do what most people had already accomplished.

I decided right then that I would put my physical pain aside and treat myself to a little outing, even if I was behind in preparations. Christmas would still come.

After convincing my husband that his John Deere suspenders and dingy looking cap were unacceptable at the theater, we headed to A Center for the Arts, a local art theater. We were treated to one of the finest hours of Christmas entertainment ever by Lance Johnson at the Mighty Wurlitzer.

The music swirled about me as he commanded the keys and the pedals to the sounds of trains, bells, drums, chimes, and music boxes. Memories flooded my soul as "Silent Night," "The Birthday of a King," and "White Christmas" were performed in all their splendor.

Shortly after we had taken our seats, an elderly gentleman with a cane sat down with some difficulty in the low and somewhat narrow theater seat ahead of us. I'd had difficulty myself. He removed his hat—like any gentleman would do—and then proceeded to eat his brown bag lunch which he had brought with him. This was okay by me. I, too, needed a diet coke in my hand even though I had gallantly resisted the powerful and tempting aroma of the theater popcorn.

His head, with a crown of white hair, began to bob in time to the beat of the music. Although I could not see his feet, I knew they must have been tapping also, as I saw his knee rising up and down in rhythm. I wondered what his story was. Who was this gentle old man who had come alone to treat himself to a bit of Christmas Spirit? Where did he live? What were his memories? Had he ever been married? Perhaps his wife was in a nursing home now, or perhaps she had passed away many Christmases ago. Where were his children or his grandchildren, and would they be joining him to celebrate the holidays?

I watched him eat his sandwich as he carefully wiped his mouth with his napkin, and I wondered how many miles he used to have to walk on his way to school. Had he been a farmer or a businessman, a teacher or a preacher? My thoughts danced in time to the music as I wondered if he had experienced the old-fashioned sleigh rides, or perhaps it was even his only means of getting to the small country church on Christmas Eve. I wondered if he had believed in Santa Claus as a child or had eaten hard Christmas candy and peanuts in the shell. I wondered if he had ever been Joseph at the manger in a Christmas play or perhaps a lowly shepherd guarding his flocks by night. Or had he been one of the wise men who were following the star and seeking the child?

The last song heralded from the Mighty Wurlitzer as it disappeared into the stage. The old man clapped his hands with appreciation of the performance. As we all did. Our hearts were filled with great joy!

The lights came on, and I watched him struggle to get out of the low, small, theater seat. I struggled from the seat behind him and gently, but firmly took ahold of his arm and lifted as he rose to his feet. He turned to my husband, who was already standing in the aisle, and said, "Thank you."

It occurred to me that he didn't know that the little boost had come from me. And that's the joy of Christmas—doing something for someone and not needing to be acknowledged for it or expecting something in return. Christmas had truly come to the old man and me in that moment. The cards and the baking and the hurry-scurry melted into oblivion. The beauty, magic and joy of the season were captured instead. I was now ready for Christmas. And I was five days early!

16

• ◆ •

Flood Waters

East Grand Forks, Minnesota is flat sugar beet and potato country. The rich Red River Valley soil is fertile and productive, and it is only two and one-half hours from where our son Mark Swenson had grown up in Fergus Falls, Minnesota. After spending his first year of teaching science and biology in California, hunting and fishing, family, and a job offer in the East Grand Forks school system lured him back to the Midwest.

In 1993, 1807 7th Avenue NW became home to Mark and wife Laurie as they became first-time home buyers. They were blessed with a son Michael in 1994. East Grand Forks continued to be good for them in the progression of life— good friends and neighbors, good jobs, and the family of God at Our Savior's Lutheran Church.

The winter of 1997 brought heavy snows beyond expectations, followed by a spring snow and ice storm. Talk of flooding was becoming more frightening. The 100 year flood occurred in 1979, so a similar one was not expected to occur in their lifetime. It never occurred to Mark and Laurie that they would be experiencing a flood far greater. Even though they thought there might be problems because of the snow, they were confident that the dikes would protect them. It would just be the usual places that might flood.

On Thursday, April 17th, Laurie left work early because rumor had it that the Sorlie Bridge was supposed to close. This was the big bridge between Grand and East Grand, and it was usually the last one to close. This turned out to be her last day of work at the Grand Forks Clinic for over four weeks.

Friday, April 18th came. Mark had already been out sandbagging for several nights. He and his fellow teacher, friend, and neighbor Jerry would sandbag until midnight. They would sleep and then go out and sandbag again. Every time Mark would come home he'd say, "It is so bad out there!"

On Friday afternoon while Mark was out sandbagging, Laurie packed the truck so they would be ready to go, packing like they would for a normal weekend to Fergus Falls. Three-year-old Michael asked, "Where's Daddy now?"

Laurie grappled for words. She finally responded, "He's with Jerry working on the dike because the river is very high, and the dike will keep the water away from our house." Trying to get his mind off the issue, she asked, "If we go to Grandma's house, is there something special that you want to take along?" He found the plastic dinosaur that his grandpa had given him, and his blanket.

At suppertime, 5:00 or so, the National Guard was going door to door telling everybody they could leave now. If they chose to stay, they should be prepared to leave at a moments notice. At times like these, it's hard to decide quickly what's most important to you. They moved things upstairs that they didn't want to lose. Sleep came with difficulty that night. They knew that the sirens would go off if they actually had to leave.

About 2:30 a.m. Saturday, Laurie was awakened by the sirens. She got up and sat in the living room and listened to the radio. The radio announcer was giving out information as to where they needed more sandbaggers and who needed to be evacuated at that point.

Laurie went back to bed after about half an hour and dozed off. At 4:30 a.m., the sirens went off again, and the police went up and down their street announcing on the loudspeakers. "Get out of town! It's time to go! The water is coming! You must go now!"

They had set clothes out earlier. Laurie woke up Mark, and they quickly got dressed. She woke up Michael and told him, "It's time to get up. It's time to go to Grandma's now."

Mark told Michael that the river was getting high and that they had to go in case it came to their house. Laurie got Michael dressed and he grabbed his blanket and his toy dinosaur.

They had been updating us regularly about the situation. It was 5:00 a.m. on Saturday, April 19, when Mark's call came. I picked up the phone knowing what the message would be—mandatory evacuation. "We're coming now. Mom, I'm scared!" I reminded him of a few things to be sure he brought along, and said we'd be waiting and praying for them.

They grabbed the box of pictures and negatives and their safe with their important papers in. Thinking they would be back in a day or two, they put out food and water for Ghost the cat—like any normal weekend.

They tried to put on a brave front so Michael wouldn't get scared. As Laurie put Michael in the truck, Mark took one last look inside the house to make sure they had taken what they needed, still thinking that they would be back in a couple of days.

Laurie was standing next to the truck with the back end backed into the driveway. She looked down the street and saw the water coming down 7th Avenue NW where they lived. She was very scared! "We have to go NOW!" she shouted. Mark came immediately. When they got to the intersection, the water was bumper high on the truck. They didn't think the water would be that deep, as it was only curb high at their place.

When they left East Grand Forks, all the streets were empty. Darkness loomed in the early morning sky, shrouding the city like an enormous cloud. The street lights were on, and they could see the water coming from side streets onto 17th Street which they were driving on. The water was flowing from west to east, and as they turned to the east the level of the water became less. Instead of taking their usual route to Grand Forks and I29, they had to go east on Highway 2 to Crookston. National Guards were at the stoplight by McDonalds where they turned onto Highway 2, dividing traffic and putting up roadblocks so no one could get downtown. More National Guards were located at the Cenex station about half a mile east. That was the last gas station in East Grand Forks where people could still get gas.

"There was one car after another," Laurie recounted. "We felt like refugees from a nuclear bomb. Everyone was leaving. It was very depressing. There was no turning back. No one was driving toward East Grand Forks."

Mark recalled, "It was kind of eerie. It was like everybody just pulled the plug and left. I don't know what it could compare to. I had never been through anything like that—total abandonment! We had been holding our emotions in for so long so Michael wouldn't be scared, but we just couldn't hold it all in anymore. We cried on the way down to Fergus Falls."

As the waters were swirling and rising around them, Isaiah 43:2 (NIV) brought them strength. *"When you pass through the waters I will be with you; and when you pass through the rivers, they will not sweep over you. When you walk through the fire, you will not be burned; the flames will not set you ablaze."*

Some roads had water right up to the edges on the shoulders of the roads. As they listened to KFGO radio station from Grand Forks, they were hearing comments about a dumpster that was circling someone's car like a shark. "It's making another pass," the announcer said!

Crookston had their river contained with dikes. They stopped at the high school there, and Mark registered so that if someone was looking for them, they would know where they were headed.

They felt reassured and relieved that they had family to go to in Fergus Falls. It was comforting to know that they wouldn't have to stay in a shelter at the air base or some place else. People ended up in a lot of strange places.

They arrived safely at our house with a hodge-podge of clothing, important papers, photo albums, the blanket, and the toy dinosaur. Although they were stressed and tired, they were relieved to be there. We hugged. We consoled. We encouraged. We cried together and laughed together.

They unpacked the truck, got settled, tried to get some rest, and began to figure out what to do next. We were all glued to the TV for news of the flood of the century and a glimpse of their home in East Grand Forks. Then we saw the fire in Grand Forks and the evacuation of people in the apartments above businesses who had not heeded the warnings to leave earlier. It was not only the flood now, but the fire too! Eleven downtown buildings were destroyed.

Saturday night Mark and Laurie realized that they would not be back home Sunday night like a usual weekend to Grandma's. A plan was made to return to East Grand Forks to access the damage, get Ghost, extra clothing, and Mark's gun collection.

On Sunday morning Mark and three other family members left Fergus Falls with two 4x4 trucks and two fishing boats, and headed back to East Grand Forks. No one knew how high the water was going to get as the river had not crested yet.

They left their trucks on Highway 220 and got in the boats to travel the rest of the way to 7th Avenue NW. The town was virtually deserted except for the National Guard. They asked them if they lived down that way, and then let them through.

Arriving at their home, the men tied the boats to the tree in the front yard and went in. Mark said that it was the first time he had ever ridden a boat to his front steps, and he hoped it would be the last.

Finding 6" of water in the basement, they felt they were staring in the face of a very serious situation. They took everything they could upstairs, including the furnace and hot water heater.

Mark called Laurie and told her that he was opening the basement windows to let the flood waters in. There was tremendous underground pressure from the water. The water was coming in between the blocks, and the foundation would crumble if he didn't take this measure. The water would have reached the main level anyway.

Now, with the boats loaded with the guns, Ghost the cat, contents of the freezer, extra clothes, etc., they headed back to the trucks and returned to Fergus Falls.

Back in Fergus Falls, friends and family pulled together to help and support. The Salvation Army and local churches were giving out cleaning supplies, groceries, and personal items. Many other families from Grand Forks and East Grand Forks had also sought refuge in Fergus Falls.

As Mark, Laurie, Michael, and Ghost settled in for three weeks of respite at our home, questions and decisions faced them daily. Would they have jobs when they returned? How much damage to their home would they find when it was all over? How would their lives change? Faith in God and prayer held them together as a family.

When they returned to East Grand Forks, they found seven feet of water in their basement. The entire basement had to be gutted and rebuilt, yet they felt luckier than some. The cleanup, rebuilding and healing began as they shared stories with neighbors and the community. Michael went to a new daycare temporarily. "The flood came to the playroom," he shared.

As Mark and Laurie reflected, they couldn't think of any reason to leave East Grand Forks. Their jobs were waiting for them. Three new schools were built, one of them being the Central Middle School where Mark still teaches science. Laurie took a job at the new PRACS Institute. In spite of the tragic experience, much good came from the flood of 1997. The town is a much nicer place. It is clean, and they have some new businesses. But sadness emerged as well. A lot of the old houses, neighborhoods, businesses, and people are gone. "After going through something like that you get stronger, and your life is better because of it," Mark said.

Now, many years later, they still worry a bit in the spring, but they feel a stronger sense of community.

Play rooms and homes can be re-built, and are, and were. Slowly their lives regained a sense of normalcy. Yes, things have changed, but they're survivors! Their lives and their spirits are strong, and East Grand Forks continues to be good for them in the progression of life.

17

• ◆ •

Baby Anna

May 1998 came in all its splendor. It was a time of promise and hope and new life. Life was not to be taken for granted. Life, indeed, was a gift!

Now it was the season of newness! Tulips were breaking through the stubborn sod, and robins were returning. I dwelt on the fragrance of wild violets and plum blossoms and walks in the woods—all these May miracles of God.

One does not think much about Christmas angels in May. But this May brought with it the announcement of a new grandchild, expected to arrive on Christmas Eve! "A little Christmas angel," I thought as my heart leaped with joy and anticipation of holding yet another new baby in my arms. "What a beautiful Christmas gift from God," I declared out loud!

Four-year-old Michael insisted that the baby would be a baby sister because they already had a brother—him!

The pregnancy progressed in a normal fashion—morning sickness, fatigue, cravings for chocolate and a growing abdomen requiring loose clothing. Soon the tiny arms and legs of this little Christmas angel fluttered softly about inside her mother's body as she performed her swimming maneuvers in her fluid environment of warmth and protection. The heartbeat spoke of new life as spring turned to summer.

Soon, the afternoon of August 18 arrived. It was ultrasound day—the day we had all waited for—waiting to hear the good news of this pregnancy.

The shrill ring of the telephone startled me. I answered. Mark's voice was soft and low, and I listened as he told me that the ultrasound results had given them some "not so good news." My heart felt pain, and tears welled in my eyes as he continued. Their baby was diagnosed as anencephalic— without a brain.

How could this be? There must be some mistake! Two days later, they were sent to Fargo for a second opinion. We met them there. We held them close and cared for Michael. The second ultrasound was completed. There was no mistake. And yes, it was a baby girl—a sister for Michael. As tears streamed down my face, I tried to make sense of what was happening.

On August 26, their little baby girl was stillborn at 9:30 p.m. I received Mark's call at 10:30 p.m. The staff had been kind and understanding. The nurses wrapped her in swaddling clothes and laid her in their arms—the only moments they would have to hold her here on earth. A baby so small—12 oz. and 10" long. They named her Anna. The nurses took pictures of Anna, the only ones they would ever have of their little baby girl.

The next day, Mark and Laurie came to our house. Laurie carried an aqua, satin covered box holding small mementos—a tiny gown and hat, a birth announcement, and film ready to be developed. She clutched a small, pink blanket—a blanket that had provided warmth for Anna's tiny body as they held her in their arms in the hospital room. But now the pink blanket was empty. It was time to tell Michael that there would be no baby at Christmas time.

Michael came and sat across from me at the kitchen table and quietly began playing with his tractors. I asked him if he would like to tell Grandma about Baby Anna. He shook his head no. I assured him that was okay and that maybe later we could talk.

Only moments went by before he began by saying, "Grandma, our baby died, you know."

I told him how sad I felt that his baby sister had died and that we would never hold her in our arms here on earth. But I also told him how happy we could be that she was now with Jesus and that some day we would see her again in Heaven.

Michael said, "She becomes invisible and goes to Heaven to live with Jesus."

Yes, quietly, Anna's soul had fluttered from her body like a butterfly emerging from its cocoon. And Michael and I knew that God was there—waiting to hug His little angel and welcome her home. I handed Michael some white paper in the shape of angels. He colored one angel with a sad face and one with a happy face, showing that he understood.

I busied myself by tenderly making a little white bonnet for Anna. It was covered with lace, ribbons, and small pink and blue flowers. I took the last few stitches now with tears in my eyes. I shopped for a soft, pink and white sleeper—so small, yet I knew it would be big on her. I found a beautiful pink blanket and a small white "blankie" to put her name on to tuck in alongside of her in her tiny white casket with the pink lining.

I was alone with my thoughts now, so I dwelt on angels. Three tiny wooden angels from Germany sat on top of my Grandma's corner shelf in the bedroom. The first angel held two candles, lighting the way for the other angels. The second angel held a golden trumpet in her hand, and the third angel carried a basket of fruit. They wore flowing, pure white dresses, and their heads were crowned with white and gold halos. Now I felt comforted that Anna was in the presence of angels and that God would also assign her a very special task. Perhaps she would carry the brightest star in heaven.

We gathered as a family in the funeral chapel. A small cascade of pink roses, baby's breath, and a small white Bible graced the top of the little white casket. A figurine of a little girl dressed in pink, encompassed by the protective hand of God, was placed alongside the flowers. Behind the casket rose a bouquet of pink and white balloons. We listened to the message of hope from the pastor. Even though our grief was worse than anything we had experienced before, we knew God was there. He would carry us through our sorrow.

At the little country cemetery, the funeral director carried the small white casket and placed it in the grave. It was a beautiful day. God had provided us with sunshine, and the sky was brilliant. Fluffy white clouds drifted peacefully, and a white sliver of moon graced the eastern sky. I held the balloon bouquet tightly in my hands and gave one to Mark, Laurie,

Michael and each one of Anna's cousins. When all the balloons were released into the gentle breeze, they floated right up to that white sliver of moon.

That night, when darkness came, I stood at my bedroom window looking at the now golden sliver of moon in the sky. And there, to my surprise, was a star unlike I had ever seen before! It was a brilliant star, cradled in the light of the moon—exactly in the spot that the pink and white balloons had drifted to earlier in the afternoon. And I knew that without a doubt, it was Anna's star!

18

◆

Observations While Waiting

I had been there before.
People milling about.
    Here and there—everywhere!
Some going up.
Some going down.
    People waiting!

Buildings. Shops. Cafeterias.
Revolving doors. Signs. Stairs.
    Elevators. Corners. Corridors.
Sirens wailing. Pagers beeping.
Cell phones ringing. Waiting rooms.
    Waiting people—waiting!

Sad faces, smiley faces, worried faces.
Bodies: tall, short, thin, stout.
    Long hair. Short hair.

Curly hair. Straight hair. No hair.
Blond, brunette, auburn and black hair.
  Waiting here!

Where do they come from?
Where are they going?
  Where is home? Where is rest?
Where is recovery? Where are the answers?
Please find the answers.
  Why are they waiting?

Carolinas. Massachusetts. Colorado. Kansas.
Minnesota. Washington. Alaska and Ohio.
  India. Europe. South America. Canada.
Kings, presidents, parents with babies.
Blue collars, business men, clergy and scholars.
  Pacing. Sitting. Waiting.

Huddled in groups. Family. Friends.
Handicapped. Agile. Chronic. Acute. Catastrophic.
  Whispers. Tears. Hugs. Silence. Breathing.
Pain. Diagnosis. Prognosis.
Fear. Relief. Anxiety. Anger. Denial. Bargaining. Reconciling.
  All are waiting.

Apple walnut scones.
Coffee. Gourmet coffee. More coffee.
  Soft music. Barely audible above voices.
Many voices. Many problems.
I'm walking alone. I keep walking. I keep asking.
  I keep waiting.

Receptionists. Information. Names. Addresses.
Ages. Birthdates. Symptoms.
　　Referrals. Walk-ins. Appointments. Insurance.
"Can I help you?" they say. My eyes dart in their direction.
I'm waiting. I'm waiting. "Please fill out this form while you're
　　waiting."
　　　I've done it before, but…I'll do it again—while I'm
　　　　waiting.

Lines of people. Medical Records. Duffle bags.
Hushed voices. Anxious voices.
　　Problems. Stories.
Faces—tired faces.
In and out. Up and down. To and fro.
　　I'm exhausted from waiting!

Unwanted bright lights.
Shield me with green plants. Hide me.
　　Time standing still.
"We haven't forgotten about you. We're running behind."
Staring…into space. I've heard those words before.
　　I know what they mean. Waiting!

Heads are nodding. Chairs become beds.
Hard wood walls and arm rails become pillows.
　　Children crying.
I need chocolate—NOW!
Color me pale.
　　I'm still waiting!

Stethoscopes in large white pockets.
Please stop and help me.
    I'm waiting!
What day is it?
Call my name.
    I'm waiting.

Is it summer?
Is it spring?
    Is it fall?
I don't know.
It could be winter.
    I've been waiting!

Next department.
Next floor.
    Go past the yellow carpet—down the left corridor.
"Please have a seat. We'll call you."
We've been here before.
    More waiting.

Old magazines. Partially assembled puzzles.
Wheelchairs. Crutches. Canes. Oxygen. Numbers. Papers.
    Waiting!
"I'm sorry, the doctors have no appointments."
"We should be able to see you in February."
    This is November! I'm hurting! I'm waiting!

Hold my hand.
I'm tired. I'm weak. I've been waiting.
    Come back tomorrow?
More hotels? Restaurants? Traffic? Schedules? Directions?
Who will see me?
    More waiting?

No more coffee. Please, no more coffee.
No more walking. No more information.
    No more thinking.
The clinic is closing.
Take me home.
    No more waiting!

19

Passage

Death knocked.
No one answered.
Tapping lightly on her door again,
death waited patiently outside the quiet room.
Quiet, except for the pumping and swooshing of
the oxygen machine.
Quiet, except for the ticking of the clock and her shallow
  breathing.

Star gazer lilies and white roses filled the room
with the fragrance of heaven.
Surely this is what heaven would smell like.
Pink walls blushed with a hint of plum surrounded her.
Would there be blushed pink walls in Heaven too?

Not quite close enough to see yet,
her body softly twitched, her fingers feeling
the satin binding on her blue blanket.
Satin. Yes, satin is what heaven would feel like.

The shrill ring of the telephone broke the silence.
She instinctively reached for the handset.
Not recognizing the Caller ID,
she laid it on her bedside table again.

Morphine dulled her pain
as overcast skies peered in her windows.
No, there would be sunshine in heaven.
She would not answer the door yet.

Sounds of grandchildren playing in the distance;
surely this is what heaven would sound like.
Caregivers entering, leaving, or sitting quietly.
They too were waiting—waiting with her
for the quiet guest to knock again—waiting for her to answer.

Death hovered at her doorway.
No, he would not enter until she was ready.
I would not leave her side.
What if she needed me?
God would not leave my sister's side either.
We watched and waited together.

Confusion shifted into conscious awareness—and back again.
Could she be remembering?
Or was she seeing something I could not see?

If death comes tonight, I would be there to hold her hand.
Transition from earth to heaven would come soon—
surrounded by the softness of angel's wings,
and the sound of a heavenly chorus.

Tomorrow I would go home.
I was torn between wanting to stay and needing to leave.
I would wait for the telephone to ring at home.
I said good-bye again—my fingers softly rubbing her arm.

I bent over and kissed her.
"Thank you for being my sister," I said as I struggled
to keep the lump in my throat from choking me;
the tears in my eyes from blinding me.
Tears in her eyes—tears in mine.
"Thank you for being mine," she echoed quietly.
I walked to the door and turned to wave. She smiled.

Days passed.
Days of suffering and pain.
Days of hanging in limbo between life and death.
Death crept softly and silently in.
No more pain. No more cancer.
No more thumping oxygen pumps.
No more nurses or shrill telephone rings.
No need to sit by her bedside.

The message came.
This time the shrill ring of the telephone was in my home.
She had answered the door.
God accompanied her to her new home,
And yet He stayed with me—holding me in His arms
as tears washed down my face.

She would wait for me beyond earth's horizon.
Someday, I too would hear the knock at the door.
I too would need to answer.
God would walk with me.

In my mind's eye, time passed.
And then I saw her—waiting for me—her hand extended,
a welcoming smile shone on her face like sunshine.

She was holding a light and beckoning me home.
Lilies and roses filled the air with the fragrance of heaven.
pink blushed walls with a hint of plum surrounded us.
Everything felt like satin—blue satin.
Sounds of children playing in the background broke the silence.
She took my hand.
Death is gone. Life is eternal. Sisters always.

20

• ◆ •

Cricket Song

Your playful tenor voice
carries through the heat of an August night.
While others sleep,
your nocturnal overture can still be heard.

Lift your majestic voice
in ode to the summer days.
Eluding people, you hide
in the camouflage of the tall grass.

Your wand waves in the summer air.
Choruses of friends join you in unison
as you conduct the concert of voices,
a gift to all who hear.

Cricket, freely serenade me with your love song
when no one else is listening.
I hear your song in the hot night air.
You stir my soul. You comfort me.

Sing in jubilant cricket praises
to your Creator!
All is still, but the Creator listens
contentedly to the sound of His Creation.

Play your fiddle, dance and sing!
Meld your repertoire in summer days.
Your chirping courtship crescendos
as you call your mate.

While other human feet dance
to stomp out your song,
I will be waiting for your encore.
So dance, elude, and sing!

Soon cool autumn nights will
steal your cricket songs.
Your pitch rises and lowers in your aria,
fading away into the night.

Surrender now your summer song to autumn days.
Your postlude succumbs in diminuendo.
I will wait through frost, snow, ice, and rain
for the new summer concert of your offspring.

Good-night cricket song.

21

• ◆ •

A is For........

Life has many interesting twists and turns as we journey around the corners. Some are devastating, some are trivial, and some are down right humorous!

I first suspected my husband was having an affair when I was driving home one evening and saw his truck parked by her place of residence close to our house. The lights were low, but visible through the small windows.

I continued into my driveway, parked my van in the garage, and went into our house. My heart was racing, and there were tears streaming down my face. This was huge!

Often he did not come home until late at night; his clothes carrying the fragrance of his lover. I begged him to spend more time with me, but he didn't respond to my pleading. He was going through his mid-life crisis. My mind began collecting more than its share of thoughts and fears.

My suspicions were heightened when new charges began to appear on our credit card bill. I knew that I had not been at any of those places.

Even his conversation with other men was indicative. He talked about the purring of her engine. I pretended not to hear. Soon I saw other men parking their vehicles by her house and coming and going at strange hours. Their wives were never with them. Even our sons from out of town repeatedly visited this mysterious lady's house—her fragrance also lingering on their clothing.

Time passed. My uneasy feelings prevailed. My husband seemed content and happy.

Finally one day, the moment of truth emerged. My husband came out of her house with his lover. He was smiling from ear to ear! She had on the most beautiful red dress I had ever seen. No wonder I couldn't compete! She was glamorous, and her eyes shone like bright lights. Truly, her engine purred with pride!

I had never seen my husband so happy, and I had never been more relieved. She was a 1945 Farmall A!

22

•◆•

Dance to Your Own Music

The old man approached me after the book reading was over. "I liked your poem," he remarked.

"Thank you," I replied.

"I just read a book about autoimmune disorders," he continued. "How are you feeling now?"

"I'm doing fine today," I said.

"No, I mean how are you really feeling?"

Perhaps, I had made a mistake in mentioning that part of my life to complete strangers when I gave my introduction. Why did he even care?

He seemed overly concerned about my well being. Did I sleep at night? Was I in pain?

The old man told me his name, but he had trouble getting it out, and I couldn't understand it. I smiled and said, "Hello! Pleased to meet you."

With crumbs of food sticking to his shaggy gray beard and a stain running from his lips down his chin, he continued the conversation. "I take tranquilizers," he said. "I'm on Medicaid," he offered freely. I responded by saying that my husband and I paid almost $900.00 a month for health insurance—that it was like a second house payment. Each time I turned to leave, he followed me with another comment or question.

His father had been a high school teacher for many years. The old man himself had graduated from Concordia College and law school. "I was the oldest one you know; my father thought I should have an education."

"Did you ever work as an attorney?" I quizzed.

"No. Tranquilizers—I'm on tranquilizers," he offered again.

Where had this man come from? Did he have a home? His long wool coat showed signs of wear—the button holes frayed far beyond the capability of holding a button snuggly. Obviously, this man was dancing to his own music!

I thought he had come alone to the book reading until he introduced me to his lady friend "Elizabeth Taylor." Far be it for me to question that! The old man felt I should know that she was into counseling "and all that," and that she was a good listener. I found it easier to talk with her. As she held a newly purchased book tightly in her hands, she told me of being a teacher for many years.

My husband wandered over for another cookie—thinking I would never be ready to get started on the one hour drive home again. He extended his hand to the old man as he smiled and said, "I'm Mr. Glori!" The old man laughed as he stumbled to get his name out again.

Perhaps this old man was where he wanted to be in life—many can't say the same. He was on tranquilizers; he would have me know—everything was good. How could that compare to the sixty pills and numerous inhalers and drops I used every day just to stay alive?

Perhaps, I was where I wanted to be in life too. I was a writer now—even though my past person had waded through a plethora of both satisfying and unsatisfying jobs. I was—for the first time in my life—the person I had always wanted to be.

I wear black. Not because I'm sad or in mourning, but because the photographer told me that someone who wears black knows where they're going. It was nobody's business that I got up in the middle of the night and sat quietly and wrote. I am the boss of my schedule, for I am the sole proprietor of my business. Job satisfaction? You bet! I can write in my pajamas, take a nap in the middle of the day, and send someone an e-mail or answer the phone without the recipient even questioning that I just crawled out of bed and my hair was standing on end. I knew where I was going! I wore black!

The old man left the building with "Elizabeth Taylor" on his arm as he tenderly called her "Liz." After all, she was a good listener you know. He was at peace with himself. He was on tranquilizers and Medicaid. He was dancing to his own music, and life was good.

I would never trade my amazing friends for anything in the world, but I can dance with myself because I've learned to be a friend to myself. And I wear black, because I know where I'm going. Life is good.

23

• ➤ •

Collections

It was a cold and cloudy early June day in Minnesota. It seemed like a good day for all to stay inside and let the weather get the depression out of its system. I had accomplished little when my husband came home from an errand and told me that the people in the red house coming into our housing development were having a rummage sale. They had had it once before, but apparently this was the final round. The dad had died, and it was "clean-out" time.

Just the sound of the words "rummage sale," "yard sale," "garage sale," "flea market," or "auction," tends to start my creative juices flowing.

I hadn't done anything to make myself presentable yet, or even eaten, but I threw on some clothes, put on some lipstick and ran a brush through my hair. Who would notice! They didn't know me. I had barely got there when it started to rain. Thank goodness I had worn my jacket with the hood.

Most of the stuff there was stuff I hope my children never have to deal with when their dad and I are gone. Stuff was dirty and old and I surely would have thrown away during the process of living. In spite of my negative attitude, I did come home with three things. One was an old half pint fruit jar—hard to find them. Then I thought, "I hope someone will want my collection of varied fruit jars when I am gone. But they will be clean." I pried the rusty cover off to see if the rim was okay and decided to buy it. Everything was half price today. I found a shirt for my smallest granddaughter. It was her size, but if it would be too long, she could wear it with shorts for pajamas. The third thing was a small aluminum teapot in good condition to add to my collection of teapots. So, I decided it had been worthwhile to go any way.

My earliest memory of "collections" was from our country church when they passed the collection plates for us to put our offering of money in. As a child, I had no idea what happened to the money put in the collection plates, but I considered it to be a very sacred part of the service. It was there that I surmised because there were two collection plates, anything I had two or more of would qualify as a collection. And so, the life-long journey of searching for the "second or more" to form my array of collections began.

I have often thought that if times got tough, I would just bring forth one of my many totes and offer the hidden wares for sale. Now who wouldn't die for an 18-gallon tote of glass insulators—every size, shape and color that had probably ever been made?

My fruit jar collection has actually been put to very good use. A variety of sizes boast various brand names and colors.

Some are dated July 14—our wedding date! A blue one serves as a vase for a few small blue silk flowers with a piece of raffia tied around the neck of the jar. Some host a home for my collection of buttons, small kitchen gadgets, tatting supplies, thimbles and old wooden containers of needles for old treadle sewing machines! I never know when I might need one of them! And where else would I display my marvelous collection of old marbles—each jar holding various colors or categories such as cat eyes, shooters, opaques, clear, and steelies.

My collections go on to include old coffee pots, china and crystal of various manufacturers and patterns—Blue Willow, Cobalt Blue Moderntone, Pink Depression, Fostoria, and Cambridge—to name a few.

To my husband's dismay, I now have an assortment of plate glass mirrors, old screens and windows stashed in the garage. Some have emerged into creative artwork and adorn a wall.

Oh, and did I forget to mention my collections of cobalt blue bottles and brown bottles and milk and cream bottles? Or how about white pitchers or cream and sugar sets?

Old family portraits framed and matted and tenderly loved line the walls of my family room. Small wooden snowmen adorn a hall wall year round. Someone made the comment once wondering if my snowmen would melt in the summer! I asked them if their florals froze in the winter!

One wall in the family room is devoted to antique metal items such as wood stove pokers and shakers, ice tongs, animal traps, rug beaters, sets of keys dangling from key rings, and bells of various kinds. I remember my deceased 80 lb. aunt when I see the very small bar bell that she used to keep in shape when she sat in her worn out over stuffed chair.

An assortment of old wooden cribbage boards is always nice. I've never played the game, but I have fond memories of my grandfather playing cribbage.

Old cookie cutters are not only decorative displayed in old glass jars or crocks, but useful as well. Categorizing is important. Gingerbread men cutters win the "most of" award. Ones with guns and holsters are worth more. Cutters with red wood or metal handles live together and ones with green handles take up residence in another container.

Lest I forget, I should mention my collections of angels, old music, old books, old wooden boxes, and old wooden duck decoys.

Yes, my house is a haven for old collections. I treasure the heirlooms that my family has so graciously given me. I am reminded daily of the character and the love of these dear people who watched me grow and nurtured me to be the person I am today.

Soon I will be having a rummage sale of my own and part with some collections and other items that longed to become a collection, but never found the second one, and I am going to part with a huge box of metal lap trays that were well used in their era. A box of glass insulators must also go. My snowmen collection needs to come down due to a pending remodeling project, but indecision still troubles me. Should I sell them or give them to a family member; that is if someone would like 35 snowmen!

So as I open totes and part with collections, I will be blessed with memories. And I will always be grateful for the little white country church that taught me all about collections.

24

'Kaffe Kjerring

At this writing, I am 36,000 feet above sea level—about 6 ½ miles high! The Northwest Airline mechanics and maintenance workers are on strike, and the Airline has filed for bankruptcy. However, I still have complete faith in the pilot!

"Cream or sugar?" asked the flight attendant. I never have put anything in my coffee. "Black please," I answered.

My thoughts turned back in time to the people who taught me to drink coffee as a child! One of my "pushers" was my Grandma Braaten.

"Oh, have just a 'skvett'," she encouraged. "Are you a 'kaffe kjerring?" she quizzed. I would giggle at her Norwegian tongue, taking pride in learning a few words from my family heritage.

In days gone by, my great-grandfather Hans Larson would sit at Grandma's table and carefully dunk his donut or cookie in the steaming hot brew. Then, he would pour some of the coffee into his saucer where it cooled quicker and drank directly from the saucer. He would have said, "Yes, please," to the flight attendant.

Growing up Lutheran in the little white country church brought a different kind of black coffee—egg coffee. The smell of coffee brewing in huge enamel pots on the wood or gas stoves in the musty basement was engrained in me. I watched in amazement as the ladies—with aprons tied neatly around their bodies—put egg in the coffee. I still don't know why a poached egg didn't emerge in someone's cup!

As I grew from childhood to adulthood, I made other observations about coffee. An old bachelor neighbor on the farm just let the coffee pot rest in peace on the stove and added more coffee grounds on top of the old ones each time he fired it up. Thank goodness, he wasn't accustomed to inviting the neighbors in for coffee very often!

Now I occasionally go to restaurants alone to collect my thoughts over a cup of coffee, and I study the people. There's the round table in back where business transactions are often made on white napkins. There are walkers stopping in for their morning coffee, and there are old, lonely people. I see little old ladies there and expect that this is the highlight of their day. I listen to their conversation which consists of little more than aches and pains, the weather, and what to order off the menu today with their coffee.

One can learn so much over a cup of coffee. As I was having coffee at the local mall coffee shop one day, I overheard a conversation—obviously a farm couple. "Well, by the time we get home, the mail will have gone!" It brought back a flood of memories, because growing up on the farm meant we governed our every move by the time of day the mail went!

Another time I was at the coffee shop, two different people made the comment, "I suppose you heard that Alyce went." Having been in grief support work for several years, I surmised that Alyce had died. When I read the obituaries that night in the local daily newspaper, I discovered that indeed—Alyce went.

Ten old coffee pots now line the top of my kitchen cupboards, reminding me of the days gone by. There is white enamel with blue trim, white enamel with red trim, cream enamel with green trim, and an array of sizes and shapes of aluminum pots. Each coffee pot has a tale to tell if one would listen closely; each pot standing firm in its own right to see all, hear all, and make the best coffee.

It seems like every time servers come to my table in restaurants and ask if they can bring me something to drink right away, I say, "Black coffee and a glass of ice water please."

To which they consistently reply, "Would you like cream with your coffee?" I guess I always thought black coffee was pretty specific, and that if you added cream to it, it would no longer be black coffee. Something to ponder.

Today, coffee is added to as many things as tempting flavorings are added to coffee. In my distant past, I made a chocolate cake from scratch that called for grapefruit juice, so I wasn't at all surprised when I started seeing recipes calling for coffee. Words like latte, espresso, cappuccino, French vanilla, amaretto, and hazelnut, enticingly dance in our heads!

I was recently notified that I had won a contest at my church to name the adult coffee fellowship time. I did a little research on the Internet on coffee and came up with a long list of ideas for entries. "Coffee Connection" was picked as the winning entry. A good conservative Norwegian Lutheran caption—a safe name—like red Jell-O with bananas and real whipped cream. Our church secretary confided in me that she actually liked my entry of "Java with Jesus" best, but she wasn't a deacon, so she couldn't vote. I guess "Java with Jesus" is a bit too perky for Lutherans—especially Norwegian Lutherans! The prize for winning the contest was, no less, a very large coffee mug.

Knowing that Jesus is always at my side, I drink my Java and smile. And as I cruise through life, I know my Savior Jesus pilots me.

The flight attendant is coming down the aisle now with her plastic bag—making her final offer to pick up the empty coffee cups and such. We will soon be landing. So keep in mind that drinking your coffee black is an option; but always trust your pilot!

25

•◆•

Traveling Companions

Rain drops streamed down the windows of the small plane as we waited to depart for our last stretch of flight home.

October, with its many and varied colors and weather patterns, was half gone. As we had waited in the airport, I pulled out the book I had bought in Santa Fe, New Mexico. I turned and looked at my traveling companion and said, "Now I am going to read to you "The World According to MISTER ROGERS {Important Things to Remember}" by Fred Rogers. I remembered as a child in rural school how I waited for recess to be done so the teacher would read a chapter from the book we were currently enjoying together. I began with the foreword written by Fred's wife and traveling companion through life, Joanne Rogers.

As I read quietly to my daughter-in-law Laurie, I was taken back in time to the days when our three children were small, loving Mister Rogers as their traveling companion.

This wholesome television program for little ones often drew me into the living room in the midst of colored blocks, small trucks, tractors, and baby dolls. We traveled through several years of life together with Mister Rogers, who assured us it was a beautiful day in the neighborhood. Mister Rogers taught children how to share, deal with anger, and even why they shouldn't fear the bathtub by assuring them, "you'll never go down the drain." Children need to know that no matter what happens in life, people who love them will be there for them. Now the kids are grown and married and have blessed me with a new audience for "Mr. Roger's Neighborhood."

There are times in our lives when a friend like Mister Rogers is needed to encourage us in the tough times, and to nurture the child in all of us. It is then that we sit amidst the colored blocks.

Our oldest son Mark—no longer "30 something"—had just accompanied his wife Laurie through the long months of breast cancer—diagnosis, treatment, and healing. He was her traveling companion through the snowflakes of winter, the blossoms of spring, and the heat of the summer, as prayers were being offered up and cancer cells were being attacked. Then the September PET Scan showed she was "cancer free." "It's a beautiful day in the neighborhood," my heart cried out! It was a "Mister Rogers Moment!" Now the autumn leaves and the good news of healing brought with them the long awaited trip to visit my sister in New Mexico. Laurie would now be my traveling companion. We reminisced about the pink ribbons adorning the chicken noodle soup cans. We were in a new season now—October being "Breast Cancer Awareness" month. The airlines were celebrating with a glass of pink lemonade for $2.00, or a can for $4.00. Yes, all for the worthy cause of finding a cure for breast cancer.

As I leaned back against the seat of the airplane, I thought about other traveling companions in my life. I thought about my granddaughter Mariah when she was three years old. One would have wondered who the traveling companion was as we walked down the open stairs. She held my hand tightly as I held on to the railing. Then she said in her authoritative, yet comforting voice, "Be very careful Grandma so you don't fall, because you would go all the way to the bottom!"

There is a child in all of us, and as we grow older, that child emerges again. One wonders at what point does the child-parent relationship reverse. When did I become the traveling companion to my mother? Was it when I began to worry about my mother's driving instead of her worrying about mine? Or was it when she rode with me and I was careful not to go around the corners too fast for fear she would tip or get jostled as she hung on to the arm rest for dear life? Perhaps it was when I helped her up the icy sidewalk to her apartment in winter or at the grocery store helping her decide which can of soup to buy when it would have been easier to have done it for her. Or perhaps it was when I scrubbed her floors, bathed her, or washed her hair. Was it when I put the spoon to her mouth and the straw to her lips? Was it when I dressed her or helped her to bed at night, or when I awakened when she called me? At some point, I stopped being the child and became the parent—the traveling companion. It was another of those Mister Rogers moments—another time to sit amidst the colored blocks.

Life is a natural cycle of giving and receiving, going away and returning, losing and gaining, sadness and joy, and living and dying and living again. It is on this journey through life that we are touched by human lives—traveling companions. Life is a webbing interaction of people needing people and friends needing friends—reaching out to each other and touching the innermost corners of the human heart.

If I am yet privileged to touch the innermost corner of someone's heart, I will set that person free to walk beside me, and I will not hold them up when they can walk alone. And if that role should be reversed someday, I would ask my traveling companion to protect and comfort me. I would ask that special person to hold my hand when I'm in danger, but set me free to feel a measure of independence still in my life. May that someone brace me with their arm when we go around the corners, and give me opportunities to sit amidst the colored blocks.

26

•◆•

God in Skin

Galatians 6:2 (NIV) *"Carry each other's burdens, and in this way you will fulfill the law of Christ."*

No one can truly see the hurt inside when outward appearances wear masks. I did not know how this story would end, but I feared it would be framed in tragedy.

January 2009 wasn't the first time we had received crises calls from our daughter in California. She had met her husband on Christian Internet 4 ½ years before, and it was an instant attraction that led to marriage. A baby girl was born to join our then 9-year-old granddaughter from Jenni's first marriage.

The calls for help came any time of the day or night; some conversation barely audible or understandable through sobbing and fear. We knew she was being controlled by her husband who was diagnosed with bipolar disorder. The air was always thick with difficulty. "If we could just be there when the storms came," we thought. We encouraged her to leave and offered our help. We fervently prayed for her and our granddaughters' safety.

Why did she stay? Was it because of her commitment before God in their marriage vows? Was it because she found security in the familiar, even though she knew she was in danger?

My prayers continued. I begged God to dance with her so she could feel the sun on her face and the wind in her hair. I prayed that He would free her from being a prisoner in her own marriage—that she could pick the mountain wildflowers and breathe the pure air that cleanses body and soul.

We learned that as parents we must simply trust God when we don't understand. "Where is God?" she would cry out—over and over again. I tried to explain to her that just when she wonders where God is, He is making the perfect plan for her life.

Now it was New Years weekend, and the calls started coming. She had finally gathered the courage to pack a few things and take her two daughters and leave the house. She was driving aimlessly around the city, not knowing where to turn or where to go. She had not slept the whole night before, and her mind and body were exhausted. We asked her if she could drive the 50 miles to the city where her dad's cousin and wife lived, but she said she didn't have the strength. We instructed her to find a hotel and check in, and we would try and send help.

Now we took the chance that cousin John and his wife Barb would even be home. They were retired and often traveled. How relieved we were when they answered the call and agreed to make the drive and bring Jenni and the girls back with them. God in skin!!

The next morning Jenni received a phone call that her husband had overdosed on medications and had been taken to the hospital ER. The doctor told her that he was getting an intermittent pulse, but didn't think he would make it.

Barb immediately took Jenni to the hospital. John got our oldest granddaughter on the plane back to Minnesota where she had been living with her daddy for the past two years. Then Papa John and our three-year-old princess left for the hospital.

We immediately started looking for flights to California. What were our chances of finding tickets for the next day at an affordable price? We were not accustomed to being snowbirds, but now needed to come as soon as humanly possible.

"God in skin" took over. We got our tickets. Our neighbor took complete charge of watching over our home—not knowing when we would be able to return. We arranged for a friend to take our van from the airport to his home.

I didn't sleep at all that night, and at 3:30 a.m. after loading the mini-van with our hastily packed suitcases, we made an attempt to leave our rural housing development. The wind howled and snow drifted our Minnesota roads. It was only January 4th, but our home town boasted nearly four feet of snow already. Winds not only made my wind chimes sing, but the wind chill was dangerous and bone chilling.

We made several attempts to get through the deep, drifted snow. Then through the blinding snow we saw lights—lights of a snowplow! The driver saw our dilemma and came immediately and cleared a path for us to get through. God in skin!

United with our daughter in California, we began the long road of healing together. At the hospital I saw our son-in-law's body swollen with drugs—only a breathing tube keeping him alive. After 72 hours of no response, the breathing tube was removed, and he died peacefully on January 6—leaving his painful past behind him.

Over and over we found that family and friends were the sweet aroma of God, and that they were His hands and feet out in the community. Co-workers and friends from their small church surrounded us with love—bringing meals and flowers and helping hands. God in skin!

Our church back home in Minnesota sprang into action. We were covered with prayer. A benefit fund was set up for our daughter and other gifts and offers of help poured in. My own life was laden with disabling health conditions, but God gave me strength to do what needed to be done at the time.

It was decided to have a garage sale before leaving. The first evening a man dressed in a business suit and tie stopped by to purchase some tools. Don't miss out on a blessing because it isn't packaged the way you expect! He visited with my husband. He came back the next day to buy more. After hearing about our daughter's situation, he told my husband that he was an estate attorney and would gladly do what he could to help her. Hired! God in skin!

Our daughter-in-law FayE flew out to California to help Wayne drive Jenni's car and Frank the cat back to Minnesota. God in skin!

On January 29, our daughter and our granddaughter and I flew back to the airport in Fargo. We hastened to get our six pieces of luggage from the baggage claim, also juggling smaller carry-ons. We were the last ones to pick up our baggage, and we seemed all alone in the small airport. Now suitcases were wheeled over to empty chairs and opened in an attempt to find the warm winter coats and boots purchased for the Minnesota weather. Almost in tears, I sat down in a chair. I saw a man walking toward us. "I thought that was you, Glori!" he said. It was our friend Pastor Kelm from our home town. Helpless as we looked, he took charge of getting our van and loaded the luggage. God in skin!

The road winds as we work to put our lives back together. On this journey through life we will continue to look for God with skin on. And we remember the words of Ralph Waldo Emerson, "Let us be silent that we may hear the whisper of God."

27

•◆•

Vang Cemetery: Resting Place

I grew up in the fellowship of the Vang Lutheran Free Church congregation of believers. Six miles northeast of Fergus Falls, Minnesota, the little white country church sat amidst the cemetery from the time it was built in 1887. The church, organized in 1884, was struck by lightning in 1939. Fire destroyed the hall and the tower and damaged the whole structure in general. The large church bell, which had resounded from its tower for so many years, was damaged beyond repair. It lay in the corner by the fence, until it was sold for scrap iron for the World War II effort. The church was immediately rebuilt. Its new steeple stood tall as it pointed to the heavens—until September 11, 1971, at which time it was set afire and destroyed—arson. I stood there in disbelief, looking at the charred, gaping hole. I had been baptized, attended Sunday School and Luther League, worshipped and was married there. But now there remained only the written history and the cemetery that surrounded it.

Earth to earth, ashes to ashes, dust to dust. Tears streamed down my face as I clung to the memories of this sacred place.

Thus, the Vang Cemetery Association was formed in 1972 to preserve the memories of loved ones and care for the cemetery located in Aurdal Township, Otter Tail County. The cemetery was first organized in 1885. The pages of the record books are now brown with age and carry with them the smell of old. My husband and I have served on the cemetery board for several years now. Wayne currently holds the office of secretary/treasurer. I hold dear to my heart this parcel of land where history and heritage now lay buried.

As I sift through page after page of cemetery records, I come in touch with family and friends who have gone before me, people who were important to me, and others I had heard of but didn't know personally. As I read, I also find others I had never heard of, but they were somebody's family member or friend. All are important to God.

I treasure some of the entries made in the old record books. On May 19, 1904, it was written, "Hartve Haugen was chosen as cemetery overseer. The grave plot dividing will be taken up at the fall meeting, and also what the congregation shall pay for a grave lot. The fee for a grave lot for an outsider would be $2.00." On November 16, 1905, the following entry was made, "Trustees to level off the graveyard and plant trees north and west of the church in the spring. Each family should bring three fence posts." And on November 8, 1961 the records stated, "A motion was made that the trustees sell the fence and put the money in an organ fund."

If I could read Norwegian, my knowledge would be more complete. As the English language became more prominent in these early years, the records turned to a strange mixture of Norwegian and English. And finally in 1939, thanks to Harold Hensvik, secretary of the church, I was able to make sense out of the records—now written in English.

I remembered Harold, a first cousin to my dad. Now buried in the Vang Cemetery, Harold (1891-1969) and Mabel (1897-1961) Hensvik, brother and sister, lived due east of the farm where I grew up by Fish Lake. Mabel was a stately, somber lady who kept a neat house and apparently knew how to sew, as I seem to remember her sewing machine. Harold was a more familiar figure to me. He was involved in the threshing crew and other shared farm activities. He drank Postum instead of coffee. We couldn't serve raspberries when Harold came to our house because the little seeds would get stuck in his false teeth. He was the tallest man with the biggest frame I'd ever seen. I didn't try to be funny around Harold. I just behaved.

To the west of us lived another brother and sister team, Adolph (1893-1971) and Pauline (1886-1952) Bergerson. Quite frankly, as a child, I worried about growing up and finding a mate since so many in the neighborhood had seemingly not had any luck in that area. I remember two things about Pauline. She broke her arm once as she reached into the mailbox to get the mail when Adolph proceeded to drive away. Then when I was about four years old and spent the summer in bed with rheumatic fever, Pauline gave me a little rubber doll with dark skin. The doll never had a real name, but I called her Brown Baby. She could drink, wet, take a bath, and occupy lots of hours. After Pauline died, my sister Jannie got to go over and clean Adolph's house and do some baking for him. Adolph liked to use the same grease to cook in for several weeks at a time and just added a few fresh coffee grounds to the old ones in the coffeepot until Jannie came over. I now own an old milk stool and a vanity bench which had been theirs. Memories.

About half way up the mile to the south of our farm lived (Paul) Oscar (1886-1975) and (Bernhardt) Bennie (1883-1963) Bergerson. I remember that they were old, bent over, and moved slowly. They gave me pink peppermints for treats so I wouldn't follow them into the bedroom to see where they kept their money when I accompanied my mother on the local charity fund drives. All these good neighbors are gone now, but the memories live on.

Many of my own family members have been laid to rest at the Vang Cemetery, including my Grandma and Grandpa John (Johan Frederik) (1872-1948) and Ose Johanna (1876-1957) Anderson. They had five children, one of whom was my father. I was only five years old when my Grandpa died. I remember very little about him except that he was old and sick and had a beard. I was thirteen years old when my Grandma died. After her funeral, I stood on the steps of the Vang Church and wept as they brought her body out to the cemetery to be buried. Grandma has sisters buried there too—Bertina Larson (1881-1960) and Theresa Anderson (1879-1965).

My dad Joseph Anderson (1913-1985) and my mom Myrtle Anderson (1914-1988) are at rest in the cemetery. I never knew my uncle Sophus Anderson (1911-1936), since he died at the age of 25 from spinal meningitis. Aunt Bella Anderson (1903-1991) died at the age of 87, and my baby granddaughter Anna Swenson was stillborn August 26, 1998.

Torgus (1839-1917) and Berthe (1850-1894) Torgusson, my great-grandparents, have one of the tallest monuments in the cemetery. They both came from Norway. Berthe died at the age of 44. Torgus was a Civil War veteran and is honored with an American Flag by his grave each Memorial Day. His Norwegian Bible rests on my library table.

After my mom died in 1988, it became my responsibility and privilege to put flowers on all our family graves for each Memorial Day. In 1989 I discovered that my other set of great-grandparents Christian (1841-1925) and Karen (1839-1921) Anderson were buried somewhere in the Vang Cemetery without markers. I surmised that times were tough in 1921 and 1925. I can only assume there might have been small wooden crosses, which rotted away with the elements of time. I have a picture of these great-grandparents that reminds me of the Cornflakes people pictured on the cereal box of old. Christian and Karen had two children. One was my grandfather John (Johan) Frederik Anderson and one was Josephine Marie Anderson. Josephine (1870-1943) married Lars P. Hensvik (1860-1944) and they had six children, two of which I introduced to you earlier—Harold and Mabel.

Christian Anderson was born in Denmark. He homesteaded the family farm in Section 12 of Aurdal Township by Fish Lake. He married Karen Kristine who was born in Norway. I don't know what her maiden name was. By myself I could not locate any marked graves for them. After some research of records and the help of my husband and the cemetery sexton Chester Holden, their graves were located in the shade of a large box elder tree on the southeast edge of the cemetery. I conducted my own little fund drive amongst the living descendents of Christian and Karen and raised enough money to have a marker placed there in their memory. Even though I didn't know them, these pioneers were part of my heritage. After the marker was placed, I sat alone one summer evening in the shade of the box elder tree. I watched the sunset and said Amen to another chapter of my life.

Over a hundred years of history and heritage are now buried in this soil. Other family names that left an imprint on my life were Twedt, Sorben, Grage, Holden, Berg, Engebretson, Leabo, Torgerson, Haugen, Oscarson and Weggeland. There are still graves that need identification and others that yet need to be found. Each one has a story of its own. The young and the old, the rich and the poor, the strong and the weak, were now sharing common ground.

Someday I will be lying beside my father in this resting place. I will share the soil with those who have gone before me. Someone will watch a sunset and remember my story or wonder what that story was.

28

•◆•

Retrospect

Today I left the small fingerprints on the windowpane. I left the toy in the corner, and the dishes undone. I rocked her extra long as she lay peacefully on my breast.

Today I held her hand as we walked the soon-to-be familiar path to her first day at school. She smiled and waved goodbye. She didn't see the tear in my eye or feel the lump in my throat. Later, I showed her the way home and listened to every little thing that excited her heart.

Today she met her first young love. He held her hand in his while his eyes spoke a thousand words of love. His future intertwined with hers as their hearts beat as one. I shared her joy. She couldn't see the tear in my eye or feel the lump in my throat.

Today was her day. A cap, a gown, a tassel! A celebration of all she had become and all she had to offer. A day of promise, new beginnings and dreams. *Where had my little girl gone?* I wanted to hold her against my breast and rock her extra long.

Today was their day. The white gown, the music, the roses, the lilies, and the love. I let go of her hand. Yet, my arms remained open. This day of joy! She didn't see the tear in my eye or feel the lump in my throat.

Today was our day. God's gift to them. Their gift to each other. Their gift to us. So small, so sleepy, so perfect, so beautiful. I took her in my arms. Her little fingers curled around mine. I was older now—a grandmother! I held her against my breast and rocked her extra long.

Today was my day. She held me against her breast and rocked me extra long. I had left fingerprints in her life. She listened as I told her of my pain. Today she was there to help me home. Today I couldn't see the tear in her eye or feel the lump in her throat.

Today she placed a rose in my hand. She remembered the fragrance of life and the bond we shared. Today she placed a white lily on my grave while she held a small hand in hers.

Today she held her against her breast and rocked her extra long. God saw the tears in their eyes and felt the lumps in their throats. He wrapped His loving arms around them and rocked them extra long.

ABOUT THE AUTHOR

Glorianne Swenson is a Minnesota-based published freelance writer, author and small business owner of **_gloribks_**.

She has been a lifelong resident of Fergus Falls, Minnesota where she grew up on a small family farm. Her career prior to writing wove around being a Registered Radiologic Technologist, Medical Secretary, Administrative Assistant, Chiropractic Assistant, After Care Coordinator for Hospice and a Funeral Home, and a Pre-school Teaching Assistant.

Her career outside the home was cut short when she acquired a disabling autoimmune disorder in 1995. It was at this time that she began her career as a writer and started her own small business *gloribks* in 2002. Her genre includes creative non-fiction memoirs, poetry, devotionals, and children's picture book manuscripts. Most of her writing is nostalgic and has been published in a variety of newspapers, magazines, and anthologies.

Glorianne and her husband Wayne have been married for 47 years. They live in a rural development on the edge of the city of Fergus Falls, Minnesota. Wayne is a retired teacher and works part time as a pre-need specialist at a funeral home. Although they kid a lot about living in "the fast lane", they enjoy being semi-retired and experiencing the slower pace of life.

Glori is the mother of three adult children and grandmother of five grandchildren ranging in age from five to sixteen. She is a member of the Calvary Free Lutheran Church in Fergus Falls.

In her spare time she enjoys singing in her church and the community, playing the piano and organ by ear, rummage sales, auctions, antiquing, genealogy, embroidery, flower gardens, public speaking, and reading her stories set to background music. Her idea of a perfect Sunday afternoon is taking a nap.